Keith Irvine

A Life in Decoration

Keith Irvine

A Life in Decoration

Keith and Chippy Irvine

THE MONACELLI PRESS

First published in the United States of America in 2005 by
The Monacelli Press, Inc.
611 Broadway, New York, New York 10012

Library of Congress Cataloging-in-Publication Data

Irvine, Keith, date.
Keith Irvine : a life in decoration / Keith and Chippy Irvine.
p. cm.
ISBN 1-58093-155-3
1. Irvine, Keith, date. 2. Interior decoration—United States—
History—20th century. I. Irvine, Chippy. II. Title.

NK2004.3.I78A4 2005
747'.092—dc22   2005017829

Printed and bound in Italy

Designed by Marcus Ratliff

Contents

To Tom Fleming, my long-suffering partner. And to the memory of my associate, George Shreyer, and my beloved assistant, Lee Barrett.

KBI

To Angela Miller, my agent for all seasons.

CI

Acknowledgments

Through the decades, I have been supported and inspired by many assistants who have gone on to establish their own decorating businesses, some becoming household names in the process: Mario Buatta, Gary Zarr, Sam Blount, Richard Keith Langham, Greg Jordan, Edwin Jackson, and Jason Bell. I am sure my present assistant, Felicity Wilde, will be a big success too. I have also been helped by talented, supportive artisans and craftsmen over the years, including John Weidl, Pat Cutaneo, Lester Drozd, Ernest Mandel, John Nalewaya, Brad Brooks, Paul Maybaum, and Tom Lent.

Chippy and I thank Suzanne Stephens for suggesting this book, Gianfranco Monacelli for publishing it, Andrea Monfried for her puissant editing, and Elizabeth White for helpful guidance. Thanks are due to Marcus Ratliff and Amy Pyle for their discriminate design—and for selecting the forthright British type by a favorite artist, Eric Gill. The photographers involved in this project deserve praise for their images; their names are listed in the photo credits. Last, but not at all least, are my clients, without whom this book could not exist.

KBI

Foreword

STEPHEN CALLOWAY

THERE IS AN old adage that when a man has done something well for half a lifetime, he should write a book about it. By that token, this book is long overdue, for Keith Irvine has now been in what he likes jokingly to call "this rotten business of decorating" for an astounding fifty years. Of course, it is a world he loves dearly, and for much of that time, he has occupied a position pretty much at the top of the tree in New York, as a founding partner in one of the city's most celebrated decorating firms, Irvine & Fleming.

Now in the fifth decade of his career, Keith is hailed as the doyen of the business—no one as fond of red and black and gold could ever really be described as an éminence grise—and he shows no sign of slowing down. His eye remains as acute as ever, and he still brings a huge rush of energy and excitement, tempered by long and hard-won experience of what works and what doesn't in the creation of interiors, to each job he takes on. Claiming to like best houses in which the mood is one of "played-down grandeur," Keith has never been afraid to pull out all the theatrical stops when the time is right. A notable example is the addition to his own Connecticut farmhouse of a vast, forty-foot-cube room crowned by a cupola; it is, he says with characteristic humor, "a room for the extremes of social life—a place in which either to be quite alone or to hold dances for which the women wear fabulous dresses."

Keith Irvine's style is unmistakable, and as a result, many of his clients have returned again and again, becoming friends in the process. Over the years, the Irvine & Fleming client list has boasted some amazing names among the rich and famous, including those, such as Jacqueline Kennedy, who were happy to be named and have their names published, but also many others, no less rich and famous, who insisted upon discretion. Nevertheless, Keith has a rich store of anecdotes spanning the years. He recalls with pleasure his student days at London's Royal College of Art, where he first met his wife, Chippy, and in particular the great influence of his first mentor, the legendary decorator John Fowler. It was the experience of working for Fowler and his indomitable partner, Nancy Lancaster, the inventors of the English country house style of the postwar years, that taught Irvine so much but that also, ironically, determined his choice to leave England forever and set up in New York.

In the many homes featured here, we see the lifework of a great decorator. Keith Irvine's vision has remained remarkably consistent over half a century. He still holds to his guiding principle that the best rooms are those that reveal "a mix of comfortable things that have drifted into your life"—family furniture, pieces of no great importance that might have come together by chance—as well as what he describes as "a sprinkling of something really super, something people can't quite believe that you have." In these pages, there are many interiors that are simple and comfortable or really quite grand, but all have been sprinkled with that "something really super": the inimitable Irvine style.

Keith Irvine in the terraced yew garden at Powis Castle, Wales.

Introduction

I WAS BORN IN Nairn, Scotland, near Inverness, in 1928 (just two years after the first "talkies" in Hollywood, the timing seemed most appropriate). The Gulf Stream ends at the Morayshire coast, and so we had beautiful benign summers. It is one of the greatest locations for soft fruit—and all those magic British gardens. In flashback, my early childhood seems idyllic: lovely empty sandy beaches, fishing for tiddlers in rock pools, freezing dips in the North Sea (as in Maine, one *knows* it is cold when the seals are swimming alongside), picnics with aspic-coated meats and kipper-paste sandwiches, daddy longlegs, and swarms of tiresome wasps.

After my kindergarten years, we moved to Aberdeen. And like Lord Byron more than a century earlier, I was sent to Aberdeen Grammar School; this was a time when French and Scottish schooling was considered the best in the world. As I was the youngest child of three and the only one still at home, my father, a relentless history buff and Jacobite, often took me along when he went to visit historic houses and castles—especially if there was a great golf course or a known trout stream nearby. We motored far and wide, visiting many great houses in the days before most of them were officially open to the public. There was a tradition (documented by the inveterate traveler and diarist Celia Fiennes as far back as the late seventeenth century) that, if reasonably dressed and polite, one could apply for entrance at the lodge, or the house itself, and tip the housekeeper, who might give a brief tour. Thus I saw many of the great Scottish piles: Traquair, Lennoxlove, Drumlanrig, Blair Castle, Inveraray, Abbotsford, Birkhall, Craigievar, and last but not least, Cawdor Castle. I was born four miles away from this last, and it would still be my favorite house in the world as a place to live in. In my dreams, I know exactly where every piece of our furniture would fit.

Opposite:
The wall above my desk.

Left and center:
I pulled together my sitting room in Richmond in 1950 on a nonexistent budget. Though the harlequin curtains and the contrasting colored walls are dated, the room embodies many of the elements I still love: comfortable seating groups, black lacquer, busts, Staffordshire figures, well-worn carpets, and always books.

Right:
The first office for the firm, then Roberts & Irvine, included a French Empire screen and chairs and an obelisk bookcase—all popular at the time. Above the mantel was a Louis XVI painted mirror (which reflects a borrowed Nattier painting), and above that was an octagonal Dutch mirror.

When I was eleven, my father was promoted to chairman of his national insurance company, and we all moved to Richmond, eleven miles from the center of London, a lovely Georgian town on the Thames. Everyone talked strangely, and the climate was pleasant—it was truly a different country. My father's and my peregrinations continued until our car was laid up on bricks for the duration: the "gathering storm" in Europe had developed as we moved into our Edwardian house. By September 3, 1939, just as I had started at a new boarding school, we had entered World War II. The war years were harsher than usual, particularly in an old-fashioned boarding school: food shortages, nightly bombings, lack of teachers, and worries about one's siblings in national service abroad created extra pressures. However, those years were oddly dreamlike, removed and romantic as old disciplines were relaxed during the Nazi bombings.

At boarding school, I met my first, and continuing, mentor, Stephen Long, the school's star art student. In our last two years, we shared a studio room in a tower. He introduced me to the fascination of interior decoration. Inspired by the then current play *Richard of Bordeaux* with John Gielgud, we created curtains by stenciling gold fleurs-de-lis onto blackout material. We borrowed, purloined, and invented furniture and objects; we painted murals. Our "style" was the cynosure of schoolboys' eyes, and invitations to our invitation-only "cocktail" parties were fought over by faculty and prefecture alike. Some were lured by the presence of my sister Willis, then a subaltern in the WRNS, who brought with her a bevy of attractive shipmates. Don't think that we didn't use this catnip to make the prefects beholden to us! More than half a century later, Stephen is a respected

London antique dealer with a charming shop on Fulham Road. Looking back over sixty years, I am still throwing rooms together—whether on a shoestring or a rather more adequate budget—just as Stephen and I threw our tower room together at school.

After World War II, I did my military service in the Seaforth Highlanders and was involved in a guerilla war against Chinese communists in Malaya. Malaya and Sumatra had a lasting effect on me. The Malays were beautiful and gentle, the country full of exotic color. From the French rubber planters, I learned how to wear a sarong—as I still do over fifty years later at summer cocktail parties.

My mother often sent me care packages. One day, returning to base camp from a jungle patrol, I received a parcel that contained the latest *Vogue* (a hopeless student through every school, I have always maintained I was educated by Condé Nast and Warner Brothers) plus, more interesting, the first English issue of *House & Garden*. Almost instantaneously, I knew that this was the profession for me. The issue included an article on four London decorators—probably all there were in 1949. I wrote to each of them from the jungle, saying, "I want to be an interior decorator." I only got one reply—from John Fowler's secretary at Colefax & Fowler, Imogen Taylor, now one of my longtime friends. Little did I know then that within a few years John Fowler would be my boss and mentor.

My father wrote to me in Malaya, on hearing of my career plans, "You can be an architect, but you *cannot* be a decorator." He had reluctantly looked into some odd "interior design" schools and took time to visit a bogus one where over-dressed debs and effete young men threw around bolts of fabric. I'm told that, describing the latter, my father growled, "They should all be horsewhipped."

When I returned to England, I found that my mother had redecorated my room—a welcome-home present. Now . . . I did not lie on the floor and kick and scream "It's *ugly!*" as Elsie de Wolfe claimed, in her book *After All,* she did under similar circumstances, but within months I started to redo it all myself. *My* way.

Helped by an army service grant, I got into the well-reputed Kingston Art School in 1950. This was a turning point, since there I met two of my best friends: the late photographer and painter John Vere Brown and the late stage and movie designer Dame Julia Trevelyan Oman, who was to marry Sir Roy Strong. After only a year there, which I spent painting pseudo–Ben Nicholsons (hot stuff then), I heard that the Royal College of Art in London was about to open a school of interior design. I applied and was interviewed by Sir Hugh Casson, the school's first professor, and, though it was a highly competitive college, managed to talk my way in.

There I met my future wife, Chippy, who was in the fashion school, though we did not get married for another thirteen years. Together, we subverted the Royal College's Ibsen-and-Chekov-influenced theater group, which was known for its formal performances as well as for its many casual "smoking concerts" and improvised entertainments—but in all cases for the *events* rather than for the acting. The three-year course at the Royal College (now it is only two years) left us time enough for extracurriculars, and we were soon writing, directing, and starring in original pantomimes, cabarets, and musicals. But for me, academically, it was a mostly wasted three years, though not for Chippy, a relentless worker and student on whom little was lost. Sir Hugh was a garrulous but generally absent teacher. I was idle, snobby, rebellious, and argumentative. I wore tailor-made clothes and drove an Allard car with an Italian body and a V8 engine—I had persuaded my father to buy it at a time when few students had cars. Most of all, I did not like the modern design directions the school advocated.

Once graduated in 1955, I again wrote to John Fowler at Colefax & Fowler, saying, with a fair amount of sincerity, "You are the only person in the world I want to work for." I have advised many people over the years to try the same ploy, since for me, it worked. During a long interview, I glimpsed his glittering world of *le haut décor*. He said, "What *have* you been doing at that college for three years? You know nothing!" I admit I almost couldn't tell the difference between English, French, and Italian chairs. My hopes were dashed when he ended the interview: "Unfortunately, we have no position here for someone like you at the moment." Three weeks later, Dame Fortune showed her face. Imogen Taylor called and asked if I could start that Monday. Tableau! A magic door to the rest of my life had swung open.

A few words about this legendary firm are in order. Sibyl Colefax was a grand social arbiter of 1920s London. After the crash of 1929, she was suddenly bereft of real money, and her myriad friends suggested that, with her sense of style, she should become a decorator. This she did, and in her ladylike, unhurried way, Lady Colefax was quite a success. A few years ago, I saw the great house Plas Newydd, which she had decorated in the late 1930s for Lord Anglesey. I was impressed because it was so amazingly comfortable, undated and smart. The house was jumped up by the romantic mural in the dining room by talented artist Rex Whistler (who was killed during World War II). Around this time, Sibyl was asked to decorate a vast London town house for Sir Alfred Beit. Unable to handle this major commission on her own, she took on a new young talent, John Fowler, to help her along. Fowler was an artist and decorator with his own small but successful business. He had a gift for paint techniques, for restoring delicate antique painted furniture, and for painting new "old" Chinese scenic wallpapers. After the Beit job—which was much discussed—was finished, Lady Colefax was suddenly swamped with new projects; panicked, she asked Fowler to help once again. Fowler agreed to do so, but only if his name was added to the letterhead. Thus a famous name in decorating was born.

The early years were fraught with difficulty—Britain was still embroiled in World War II—but not surprisingly, it was a time of great design ingenuity. The fabric shortages imposed during and after the war inspired curtains made from army blankets (as at Clandon), slipcovers made from the pink-and-white-striped cotton used for nurses' uniforms (long before ticking became a fashion fabric), and the use of *noil,* or the silk waste left after making parachute cloth. One of the firm's clients was Mrs. Ronald Tree (née Nancy Langhorne, and soon to be Nancy Lancaster), a wealthy American grande dame and dilettante decoratrix, who became frustrated with the length of time Colefax & Fowler spent on her project. Her solution? She bought the firm. Nancy slipped in as Sibyl Colefax slipped out, becoming a hidden but far from silent partner. She rounded up her wide circle of acquaintances as new clients and fast gave the firm the style and clout it still carries today.

And John Fowler? He was a brilliant, dedicated giant, obsessed with detail and accuracy; a severe taskmaster, part charmer, part fiend. From a sympathetic smile, his steely gray eyes could turn to ice on a dime if one overstepped one's mark. He was also an inspired teacher; sometimes he would dump an appointment with one

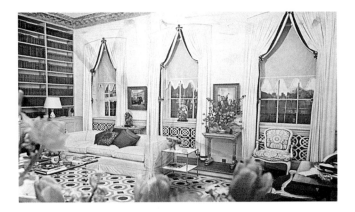

of his duchess clients and whisk me off to the Victoria and Albert Museum where his overloud explanations would embarrass me to death. When traveling on distant jobs in the old Daimler with Wilson the chauffeur, Fowler would explain architectural details on buildings we passed. On the way back—horrors—he would quiz me, and there was thunder on the horizon if I flubbed my answers.

What a whirlwind apprenticeship—part paradise and part reign of terror! I sure felt I earned my *very* meager stipend. The quality of the houses he worked on and the originality of his decoration were unsurpassed. He was a magician with color and painting, experimenting with new and rediscovered paint techniques. He reinvented the clear, lively tones that had disappeared for over a century under the somber fussiness of the Victorians and Edwardians.

From his looks and manner, one would never have guessed he was a decorator. In his plain tweed suits and subtle ties, he looked more like a learned county lawyer in town on family estate business. He chided me when I appeared for my first Colefax & Fowler Christmas party wearing an extravagant pink silk tie and matching socks (Turnbull & Asser) with my one gray flannel suit. And smoking pink Balkan Sobranie cigarettes! "Our profession is always the butt of innuendo and gossip, dear boy," Fowler commented. "Don't give them unnecessary ammunition."

He was at heart a scholar and researcher. Lifting veils from the past in the decorative arts fascinated him. This was heightened by Nancy Lancaster, that indomitable Virginian. Along with Charles de Beistegui, they were perhaps the greatest pair of dilettante decorators of the twentieth century. Mrs. Lancaster had just bought her last great house, Haseley Court in Oxfordshire, when I first joined the firm. Earlier, at Ditchley Park in Oxfordshire, she had riveted *le monde du décor* by making a big-as-a-palace James Gibbs house vibrant and comfortable, though she did have some professional input from Parisian master decorator Stéphane Boudin. The bathrooms, lavished with books, flowers, porcelains, and enticing chairs, were apparently a revolution in their inspiration. She had an innate gift for unexpected furniture arrangements and a knack for taking grand pieces and situations down a peg. One of her most quoted observations was "Decorating? I'm agin' it."

Nancy Lancaster and John Fowler were a formidable team, he with his erudition and she with her flair—and money. It was an inspired love-hate duo. They energized each other, and their spats and quarrels were the stuff of legend, earning a famous epithet from Mrs. Lancaster's aunt Nancy Astor: "the most unhappy unmarried couple in London."

For Colefax & Fowler, their relationship was a bonanza. Mrs. Lancaster's rich and fancy American friends, envious of her ravishing great houses in the incomparable English countryside, fast bought great houses themselves and signed up with Colefax & Fowler. They began, thrillingly for them, to entertain members of the British aristocracy, who in turn realized that their even greater hereditary piles could be as stylish and comfortable as the seats of these upstart Yankees. Gradually they too made their way to our office on Brook Street: there were eight English dukes on the books in my time. The cash registers were ringing and the "English country house look" off and running. (It is important to note that the English country house look was accidentally and subconsciously invented, evolving naturally from Mr. Fowler and Mrs. Lancaster's instinctive genius and unswerving convictions.)

For me, these years were a dream of hard work and phenomenal rewards. The houses and clients were extraordinary, though I never felt secure or comfortable in such rarified circumstances. I came from a middle-class family and had not gone to a top-flight public (in the English sense, that is) school. In those pre-Beatles days of the 1950s, the class system in Britain was strong and seemed unchanging. In many ways, it *still* is. I believed I could never climb to the executive level at Colefax & Fowler.

Luckily, at this moment, Mrs. Henry "Sister" Parish II was in London sizing up—as she did three or four times a year—what Fowler and Lancaster were up to. She was working on a big house in Johannesburg for the wealthy American Engelhard family, and everything had to be ordered and bought in pounds sterling. Sister Parish was confused by English finances and how orders were processed, and so Fowler lent me to her to organize the job. When the house was completed, she asked if I would come and work for her. New York and forty dollars a week sounded alluring. I was uneasy about my future in London; both my parents had died; and a great buddy and Colefax girl, Caroline Harford, was going to the United States for an extended visit, so I would have a friend. Sure, I'd try it for a year. That was in 1957, almost fifty years ago.

I was seriously hard up, and so I traveled on a freight steamer. When we finally glimpsed the lady and her torch, it was too late to dock, so we lay out in the outer harbor. All night I stood on deck, fascinated and horrified by the lights of automobiles pumping incessantly round the edges of Brooklyn. Where would I lay my head tomorrow night?

I had only thirty-eight dollars to my name. If I ever mention that to my daughters now, they take out their imaginary violins and start playing schmaltzy music. The next morning, I took a cab straight from the steamer to Sutton Place, the home address I had for Mrs. Parish. She was not "down" yet and I had a nice breakfast with Mr. Parish, but from the way I was questioned I realized that Sister had forgotten she had hired me. Later, in the office, the situation was further aggravated; I was handed a postcard from a friend in London that had obviously made the rounds: "Lord help the Mister who comes between you and Sister."

It was not a happy situation. I realized I did not like Mrs. Parish—and the feeling was mutual. I was the only guy among all these gels. They wouldn't let me use "their" bathroom, and I had to go across the street to the Old Westbury Hotel. Sister used me as a shopper, whereas with Fowler, I had been doing whole houses. (The spring and summer before, I had decorated a flat in Eaton Square for Sir Laurence Olivier and Vivien Leigh as well as their country house, Notley Abbey in Buckinghamshire.) I was not impressed with Sister's decorating, which

was appealing on the surface but without depth. She had little interest in the bones of our profession: interior architectural detail. I stuck it out for nine months, then left under a cloud. Sister's parting words were "You will never last for a year. You don't *know* anyone."

Shortly after I arrived in New York, as I searched for an apartment share in the *New York Times,* I had met a larger-than-life character who called himself Robin Roberts. (His real name was Robert Schwaid.) He was then working in the mail room at the giant advertising agency J. Walter Thompson and in the evening taught the cha-cha-cha at a Fred Astaire Dance Studio. Quick as light, he caught on to my profession, and to the power of John Fowler's name. Before I knew what was happening, I was a partner in a new decorating firm, Roberts & Irvine, with an office we couldn't afford on the Upper East Side.

Six months along, we had two great clients who had drifted my way from Sister Parish, and suddenly we were busy enough to need an assistant. Again from the *New York Times,* we found Tom Fleming. He was hardworking, sincere, and movie-star handsome. For over forty-seven years he has been with the firm, a reliable partner and, next to Chippy, my staunchest friend.

On February 16, 1961, Bob Roberts (as I called him) and I launched a new fabric company, Clarence House. We drew upon my know-how around French and English textile mills and Bob's astounding chutzpah. It was a success from day one, but before the year was out we had split, Bob taking Clarence House and I the decorating firm, renamed Keith Irvine & Co. As our clients became more top-drawer, Bob had become a liability. He didn't move readily in "polite society,"

Left:
This early job, in Watch Hill, Rhode Island, was for Tina Barney. The assemblage of abstract paintings, Le Corbusier Petit Confort armchairs, old Orkney chairs with woven-rush backs, and bold Navajo rug suited the open plan of the house.

Center:
Vita Sackville-West's writing room, on the first floor of the tower at Sissinghurst, was an intimate mix of past grandeur and unpretentious rusticity. The room seemed to have decorated itself, which I found inspiring.

Right:
The ink blue library for Mrs. John Sherman Cooper had rough dragged walls, dark blue Fortuny fabric, bold antique Chinese rug, Salvador Dalí sketches, and Mrs. Cooper's own superlative English mahogany furniture.

Left:
In the early 1960s, Irvine & Fleming decorated a small cottage in the Hamptons for the bon vivant bachelor Serge Obolensky. Despite the tight budget, we injected a spirit of high style that reflected his lively social life, even as an octogenarian.

Center:
One of the most glamorous jobs of the early days of the firm was a mansion in Palm Beach for Aimée de Heeren. The Indienne fabric in this large drawing room is from Lelievre in Paris.

Right:
The main living room in Lydia Melhado's beach house in the Hamptons was a sea of white wicker with a strong blue and white print of Chinese pots; David Hicks copied the design from an old watercolor he had found in Wales. The white flokati rug and sectioned painting of an artichoke seem dated now, but in the early 1960s, we thought they were the cat's whiskers.

whereas Tom Fleming, who stayed on with me, had that admirable, unabashed American confidence and was at ease among icons such as Katharine Graham, Governor Averell Harriman, and Alfred Gwynne Vanderbilt. (At one point in the mid-1960s, we worked for almost every member of the Kennedy clan.) Tom gradually moved up and became a partner on January 1, 1967. Bob Roberts, with his entrepreneurial talents, went on to make Clarence House a household name internationally.

For the next four decades, our traditional mode of decorating developed but never really changed, despite the shelter magazines' and most of our competitors' design swings through Italian modern, English country house, Scandinavian stripped-down pine, postmodern, high tech, overrich opulence, shabby chic, and high-priced minimalism. We went on producing personal, comfortable rooms, very few without a sprinkling of English and French chintzes—always our favorite fabric, and one our type of client understood.

Looking back on over half a century in my profession, I can see that, though my strengths have always been traditional and English (albeit with one foot in France), they have developed as the world has changed. We are all influenced in some measure by Dame Fortune. After I came to the United States, my on-site education was inspired not only by American history but by new ideas and materials. John Fowler and Nancy Lancaster were the most forceful mentors of my style, yet two talented friends of my youth, Stephen Long and John Vere Brown, were deeper, longer-lasting inspirations, leading me to a relaxed, more theatrical view of Englishness and its suave eccentricity.

My style might be better summed up by two outside observers. The late Valentine Lawford wrote about Chippy's and my house in *Architectural Digest* in March 1980, "As in the work of Fowler, so in the work of Irvine. It is rather easier to list the ingredients than to describe the dish. Superlative English and French furniture and carefully oiled and preserved leather-bound books, many flowered chintzes, needlework carpets, animal portraits, quilts, a touch of tartan and a twist of Gothic—one and all play their role in the interior of the Irvine farmhouse." In the 1989 book *Colefax & Fowler,* author Chester Jones wrote, "Keith Irvine, one of America's foremost decorators, a witty and somewhat iconoclastic designer, has achieved a style very much his own. His whimsical use of nineteenth-century furniture and fabrics has a richness of pattern and warmth that envelops one like Mr. Dick's hospitality in Dickens's *David Copperfield.* His deliberate mixing of furniture styles, and the jumble of bits and pieces of china, prints and needlework evoke something of John Fowler before an editing has taken place. His wide use of chintz has helped prepare the American taste for it."

Throughout the years, throughout the projects, I have relied on the support, spirit, and honesty of my partner, Tom Fleming. On we will go and on we will decorate, I suspect until we are carried out in a box. In a way, it will be the final fade-out for the long Fowler legacy, though I know we will both hold the curtain open for as long as we can.

Rural Hideaways

I FIRST MET the Bortz family through George Shreyer, a gifted but tortured young designer who worked as an associate at my firm in the early 1960s. He, Tom Fleming, and Mario Buatta were the most shining design talents to pass through the Irvine portals in my long career in America. Though I was the boss, I was constantly learning from their natural (not school-bought) artistry.

George was charming, inspired, 150-percent enthusiastic, but he had a deep psychological flaw. He would stay up all night, pushing the social whirl (Jackie and Lee Bouvier were always at his parties), his mind whizzing with creative thoughts, and then he would be unable to come to work in the morning. The daylight scared him. By four in the afternoon, he might be brave enough to surface. He was a real sweetheart (one of his charms was that he taught Chippy how to drive in New York City), but impossible to handle. God knows, we all tried.

The situation deteriorated, and one night he took a room in the then recently opened New York Hilton and committed suicide. In the eleven-page goodbye letter he left for me, he included not only a sketch design for his neo-classical headstone but also a forceful admonition to Tom Fleming, then young and wide-eyed, to travel—Europe, *Europe,* EUROPE—with a sketchbook! What a terrible waste of talent. By now he might have outpaced all of us to be the twenty-first century's Billy Baldwin.

Pennsylvania Manor Farm

George had become friends with Richard Bortz at Princeton and had helped him with an eighteenth-century stone farmhouse outside Reading, Pennsylvania. By the mid-1960s, Bortz was married with three children—there would be six—

Opposite:
Frances and Richard Bortz—at one time master of the hunt—on horseback in front of their Pennsylvania farmhouse.

and in charge of his family's chocolate-making business. He enjoyed being called the Chocolate Bunny, even when he was master of the hunt. Frances Davidson, his bride, was strikingly attractive, unsurpassed in an evening gown or a black Hermès riding habit. She was an East Coast, old-money, WASP princess. Richard was handsome in a rough kind of way, audacious at times, though super persuasive when the moment suited him. A young James Mason could have played him at the drop of a hat. No wonder that when Chippy and I put on a pseudo-Shakespearean masque in our garden, Richard played Henry V—and he arrived from Pennsylvania in a helicopter, bursting with energy and full of fun and larks.

Richard was the one in the family truly interested in interior decorating; Frances preferred her hunting and horses, although she politely agreed to our ideas and suggestions. Richard, who saw himself as a born-again Charles de Beistegui, had great plans for expansion and gradually bought up every surrounding property in the valley.

The entrance hall was my first serious step into valued American traditions. Simple and bold with an echoing marble floor, it had plain white

An unpretentious American farmhouse hall with uncomplicated white walls and dark green trim. Furnishings include a Queen Anne hall table and a rococo Venetian side chair, once painted but now stripped.

walls and an old oak-leaf wallpaper border. Most striking were the doors and wood trim, all painted in dark bottle green. This continuation of a northeast American custom absolutely floored me, with my English background: it was so unpretentious and clean, like the best American traditions.

Richard, armed with a rough sketch drawn by George Shreyer on the back of an envelope, had planned to build a ballroom plus a new wing three times the size of the original farmhouse. (Could this have subconsciously inspired me to build our ballroom some thirty-five years later?) We worked with the Bortzes and a local architect, William Kirkpatrick, to create a clapboard building with some stone elements that would flow out of the old stone of the original farmhouse. The ballroom, a tribute to George's ideas, was grand and two floors high. Pale glazed walls were interspersed with painted wood pilasters, faux-marbled rather crudely to look as if an itinerant, unskilled Italian craftsman had painted them in some imaginary country palazzo. The geometric floor was also faux-marbled, but in a specific neoclassical design that mimicked a Portuguese needlepoint rug owned by the Bortzes. So they had a great rug in the winter and a similar-looking great wood floor in the summer.

The vast tray ceiling was covered in an anaglypta "plaster-style" design. Anaglypta is a cardboard-paste molded product that, when stapled in place,

In the private sitting room are an eighteenth-century Scottish pine mantel and two cozy sofas slipcovered in a peacock blue Fortuny fabric.

In the ballroom is a large painting of Frances Bortz with her mother and siblings. The sofa in the portrait is still in use in the farmhouse.

spackled, and then painted and glazed, looks just like real, old hand-plastering. Down from this ceiling swept a gargantuan gilded carved-wood and gesso eighteenth-century Austrian chandelier. It was never wired but had real candles, which I love. The Bortzes also loved it, especially as it gleamed for their parties. It was set on a mechanized winch so the candles could be replenished.

Most of the furniture in the room came from the old Davidson house on R Street in Georgetown in Washington, D.C.—also a house with a ballroom.

26

Some pieces were re-covered; some retained their original finery. Crazy Edwardian stuffed chairs in the olive green velvet of the old Davidson ballroom looked as if they had wandered in from a production of *Lady Windermere's Fan*. A black Regency chair had been purchased by Richard from Irvine & Fleming for twenty-five dollars in 1962. (As a polite gesture, he always bought something when he came to our office, as English clients tended to do when they visited Colefax & Fowler. I have always regretted selling it for so little!) A large sofa was covered in the chinoiserie print Le Lac,

Two Hepplewhite country chairs covered in antique (but not original) crewel embroidery flank a William Kent cabinet. The nineteenth-century Italian plaques depict Roman emperors.

the very first time I used it. In those days, we bought it from Rose Cumming, though it is now sold in the United States by Brunschwig & Fils. Above the big sofa was a portrait of Frances with her mother and three siblings. The settee on which they were posed was re-covered and used in another room in the farmhouse.

There was a great *faux bois* early-eighteenth-century cabinet Richard and I found at the late Eleanor Merril's shop; like one belonging to Chippy and me (see page ooo), it was by William Kent. Eleanor Merril, though not conspicuous, was the doyenne of New York *antiquaires,* a truly Dickensian character with a lightning-fast eye for the unusual. Chippy always described her as "the last of the good witches." I first met her in London, when I was working for John Fowler and she bought some antiques. Quaintly, she tipped me two pounds (in 1956, this was close to my weekly salary), and she became a mentor. Ms. Merril, who *never* suffered fools gladly, warmed the cockles of my "limey" heart when she ordered the omnipresent Sister Parish—that juggernaut of dictatorial decorators—to leave her shop and to please never darken her doorstep again!

In addition to the ballroom, the new wing included a master bedroom suite with a lovely, much lived-in private sitting room. It looked beguiling—and as if no

In the dining room, an American sideboard covered with Richard's collection of antique Worcester china.

decorator had been near it! The components were, and still are, timeworn: old rugs, old Fortuny damask, and English printed linen called Hollyhock. The one new element was the first English printed honey-colored strié wallpaper I ever used, bought from Cole & Sons in London. A neat idea was an alcove built in front of a window to hold an antique French daybed with interior bookcases at either end. It was partly hidden by the Hollyhock curtains and so was ideal for afternoon naps—or even for nighttime if one's partner had a headache. The room could have been in the grandest house but was played down to perfection by both the clients and myself.

The house wandered on through many children's bedrooms and guest rooms. In the older part of the house was a homey dining room—the kitchen of the original eighteenth-century house. It glows with burnt orange paint-glazed walls and a gallery of family portraits commissioned from Aaron Shikler. (He painted

Upstairs in the barn is a dining area used for parties. Painted Italian chairs surround the table.

the famous portrait of Mrs. Kennedy in the White House.) A lovely old American paneled study nearby was painted to look bandbox fresh.

Not far from the house was an old barn, which we restored and rearranged on two levels to be a guest house, or a great party barn. We retained the rough spirit of the barn structure; outsize windows let in light and views of the countryside. Striped canvas curtains separated different areas but could be looped back to add a theatrical touch. A sophisticated background to the dining area was an antique Dufour scenic paper called "Brazil." I can vouch for some of the many rollicking parties held there!

Even when the job was finished, or as finished as this kind of house can ever be, I used to visit the Bortzes a couple of times a year for a jolly drunken dinner and some great 1930s syncopated music—Richard adored Fred Astaire and

29

Opposite:
Nautical architectural details were added to the former fishery in 1917, when the building became a summer place.

Ginger Rogers. We would move furniture and rehang pictures into the small hours. The best fun any decorator can have is this kind of playtime with stylish clients, reinventing rooms in an instant.

A Summertime Galleon

Richard and Frances Bortz also owned a remarkable summer place in North Haven, Maine, an island eight miles out in Penobscot Bay. Built on the shore of North Haven's harbor around 1870, the house had belonged to Frances's parents; before that, it had been a fishery. In its extraordinary present form, dating from around 1917, the house appears to be the aft end of an old galleon, half in the water, and is approached from the dock by a gangplank.

Sometimes called the Fish House or the Ship House by the locals, it is a marvelous vacation house, casual and a bit primitive but crammed with atmosphere. There was not a stick of decent furniture in the place; it was full of the detritus of generations of happy, shoes-off summers. Yet one ate off eighteenth-century Canton china, and the sunsets with drinks on the poop deck were game, set, and match! We re-covered some odds and ends but did not do much in the way of decoration.

Richard died far too young, leaving a cloud of loss over family and friends. He sailed off, literally, into a Maine sunset, dying of a heart attack during a solitary late-afternoon sail (probably with a flask of martinis), but in a place he passionately loved. What style that man had! My mind still turns and says, "Oh, I must tell that to Richard!"

Blue-and-white china—some of it real Canton—on a simple white pine table in the dining room.

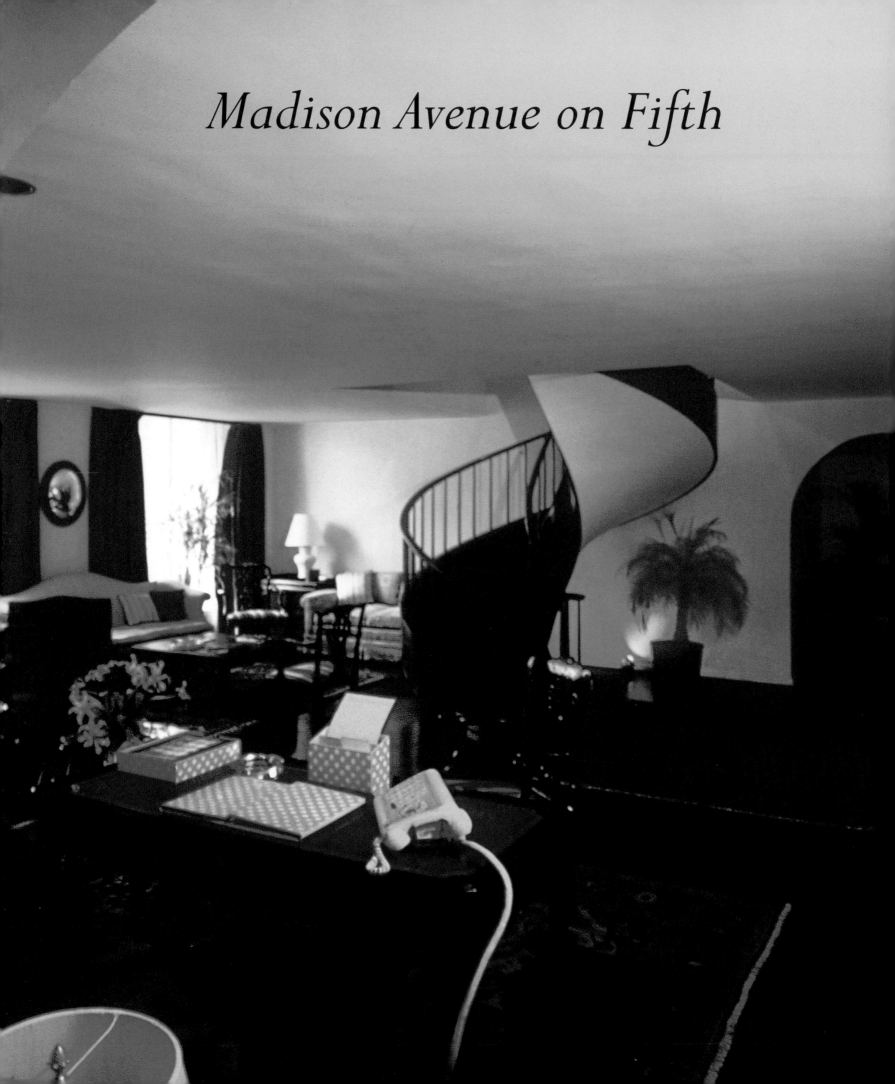

Madison Avenue on Fifth

I MET THE legendary Mary Wells in the 1960s when she ruled the decade's cutting-edge advertising agency, Wells Rich Greene. The company had just leased two floors in the brand-new General Motors Building on Manhattan's Fifth Avenue. Stylist Nancy Reals—who advised Mary on fancy clothes because she was simultaneously speeding up the social ladder—landed Tom Fleming and me the biggest job we had ever had.

We almost never got to see Mary Wells directly. She was far too busy, and she was also romancing Texan millionaire client Harding Lawrence; she famously transformed his airline, Braniff, by painting the planes in technicolor rainbows and dressing the stewardesses (as they were called then) in Emilio Pucci miniskirts and boots. All our work had to pass through a posse of handlers. We got to see Mary (and Dick Rich and Stewart Greene) only when we had large "show and tell" presentations.

We worked on the project with architect Robert Liebreich—the first of many collaborations. Though the overall design was formal, we also focused on the dramatic. In addition, Mary insisted on fine details, already a hallmark of our company. The walls of the main elevator lobby were covered in thick, shiny, Chinese red lacquer with a hand-rubbed and -polished wax finish. The treatment was grounded by dark bronze elevator doors and dark, bronze-tinged trim. Geometric David Hicks carpeting covered the floor. I think we forget nowadays what a worldwide design influence he was in the 1960s. He picked up elements from America's love of spirited, clean ideas; took them back to London, where he refined and redefined them, adding European flair; and sold them to the world. For two decades, his carpets covered (or so it seemed) almost every floor in Europe and America.

The bright red of the elevator lobby was echoed by simple but lush silk taffeta curtains in the reception area. The space was furnished with a comfortable, eclectic mix of overstuffed pieces—a big, serpentine-topped Chippendale settee, "comfortable enough" antique chairs and tables, antique Oriental scatter rugs on a parquet wood floor, and pretty lamps and cushions. The most spectacular design element was a sinuous spiral staircase sweeping up to the next floor.

Above and opposite:
A dramatic freestanding spiral stair, part of the design from the earliest sketches.

Double doors flanked by matching architectural bookcases at either end of Mary Wells's office.

Mary Wells's office was, like her, cool, blond, and svelte. The walls were strié-glazed in pale pink champagne; luxurious yet simple curtains, made of heavy Roman satin, were a deeper shrimp color. The palette of the bold antique Sultanabad rug was coral, beige, and ink blue. An English Radcliffe sofa in dark chocolate brown mohair velvet added gravitas. The double doors at either end of the office were flanked by matching glazed architectural bookcases. We painted them a darker coral inside, an old decorating trick that increases the feeling of depth—and it looks rather pretty.

Mary's office led to the boardroom, a large corner space looking out onto spectacular views of the Plaza Hotel and Central Park. A third of the room was split into seating groups for small or casual meetings. In the larger area was a more formal, English table surrounded with Chippendale-style chairs; the ensemble was softened by an antique Oriental rug. The curtains were made of an unusual quilted blue and beige English cotton print with a Gothic-inspired design. Off to one side, a tiny conference table surrounded by French Directoire chairs was backed by a screen of hand-painted Chinese scenic paper made by Gracie & Sons in New York.

To the side of both the boardroom and Mary Wells's office was a tiny hall that led to a powder room and a bar. The mirrored hall, with a decorative French mirror in the Egyptienne style and a French Empire console, complete with asp slithering up one leg, had a French Directoire feeling. The bar was more 1960s glass and chrome modern; an unusual French Empire *papier-peint* screen, called "Monuments de Paris", and two antique fruitwood Louis XV *bergères*—by great good fortune still covered in their original tan leather—gave it a sharp Gallic edge. A modern vein ran through the rest of the offices. Mary insisted that we interview her "star" cohorts so that we could inject individualized thoughts and interests.

Our final installation took two weeks at a rather fast clip. The next day, Mary Wells called us and said, "It's terrific! But it looks as if too much money has been spent. Take everything out of the executive offices and put it in storage. Let's re-form it in an inexpensive-looking and spare way. You can just put packing crates in my office!"

Though the job had this depressing ending, a lot of the furniture crept back in over a period of months. Gradually, I became aware that the very best things did *not* reappear; it wasn't until a few years later that we noticed them in magazine photographs of La Fiorentina, the famous villa in the south of France that Mary and Harding Lawrence (by then married) had bought. Tom once asked Mary what she would do when she retired from the Sturm und Drang of advertising, and she answered, "I will have many of the most beautiful houses in the world." She ended up with six—one in New York, one in Dallas, one in New Mexico, one in the south of France, one in Mustique, and one in London. Mary was almost the equal of our all-time householder Drue Heinz (Mrs. H. J. Heinz II); when we first worked with her, she had nine fully staffed houses around the world.

The final chapter of our work for Mary Wells Lawrence followed apace. One Friday, Nancy Reals asked me to join Mary for a drink at her Gracie Square apartment. As we talked, she told me that she and Harding were going to Acapulco the next day to look at a house. Would I come? (I guess the odd Braniff plane was always on hand.)

Unthinkingly I said, "Oh, I never work on Saturday!" Six of the most unprofessional (and untrue) words I have ever uttered. Nancy Reals told me later that after I left, Mary telephoned Billy Baldwin. He flew to Acapulco with her on Saturday, and he proceeded to decorate four of her six houses. And beautiful jobs they were (as always). Toward the end of Baldwin's career, he called Mary Wells his most inspiring client ever. Stupid old Keith! 🐱

Louis XV *bergères* and a 1960s chrome and glass table in the bar. Against the wall is a *papier-peint* screen with scenes of Paris.

Democratic Dream Houses

JOAN BENNETT KENNEDY is a sweet, thoughtful woman, and a blond American beauty. Her smile and sparkling charm won many hearts in the Camelot years of the early 1960s. Always somewhat shy, she was supported in the Kennedy family maelstrom by her buddy Jackie Kennedy, who let her know it was better to follow her own musical bent than to play touch football with the in-laws. Jackie also recommended me to Joan and Senator Edward Kennedy as they were building a new house overlooking the rapids of the Potomac River in McLean, Virginia, for their growing family.

Family House in Virginia

The house, designed by architects John C. Warnecke, a Kennedy groupie, and Peter Sayer, was a sprawling spread centered around a two-story, barnlike great room. Senator Kennedy, a charmer like his wife and the youngest of the dazzling Kennedy brothers—wow, were they ever dazzling!—was not too involved beyond the first two or three planning sessions, but Joan was deeply into every detail.

The house's reception rooms—entrance hall, great room, library, and dining room—were designed to enhance a wealth of fine antiques. These were mostly American pieces from the 1964 Karolik sale in Newport, Rhode Island (the bulk of the collection was acquired by the Boston Museum of Fine Arts). The couple also owned a lot of good English antique furniture that had originally been purchased by Ted's father, Joseph Kennedy, to furnish Winfield House in London when he was ambassador to the Court of St. James.

I worked on the project with Tom Fleming, who had just become my partner, and my beloved assistant, the late Lee Barrett. Our goal was to create an eclectic,

Opposite:
In the center of the entrance hall, a George II "rent" table with multiple drawers under a Dutch chandelier.

In the living room are an English rococo mantel, a George III partners' desk, and Joan's grand piano.

sunny background. In addition to the reception rooms, we worked on a wing of childproof rooms for "the kids." Never barred from the main rooms, they did have their own territory.

The entrance hall was centered around a spirited antique English George II "rent" table. Such tables, often circular in shape with multiple drawers inlaid with letters in alphabetical order, were placed in the halls of English manor houses. Once a week, the landowner would sit beside the table and receive rent from tenants; his agent would stash the receipts in the appropriate drawer. The Kennedys' rent table sat under a central dome with a complementary brass Dutch chandelier. On the floor was a bold geometric antique Serapi rug from eastern Turkey; its tones offered the first hints of the color palette of the great room beyond.

This space, the main living room, was divided into a series of interlocking conversational groups. The high ceiling was crisscrossed with massive old beams that nurtured a story—patently untrue—that has ricocheted through the years ever since. We, along with our clients, had decided that the beams should be whitewashed to accentuate the light, airy flow of the space. But Maxine Cheshire, then the terror of Washington society, wrote about the newly decorated house in the *Washington Post*. On first seeing the whitened timbers, she said, Ted Kennedy had thundered, "Okay, who is responsible for whitewashing my old beams?" Teddy knew vaguely of the whole plan, but this oft-repeated myth has dogged me for the last four decades, and by now I am used to seeing magazine pieces full of evasive and fabricated—but dramatic—details.

The walls of the room were strié-glazed in a bright Giverny yellow that played off against bold Chinese red taffeta curtains. These simple curtains helped divert the eye from the large, ugly, 1960s plate-glass windows overlooking the bluff down to the Potomac. The room was also humanized by a vast antique Ushak rug in soft, sun-faded colors. Ushak, Samarkand, and Sultanabad

Oriental rugs always work fabulously with Western furnishings. In the eighteenth and early nineteenth centuries, these carpet-producing areas created rugs in designs and color ranges that were intentionally less ethnically Islamic and more readily acceptable to Western taste; and they suited softer European painted rooms and furnishings superlatively. Also in the Kennedy great room were a rare English rococo pearwood carved mantel—the only one I have ever come across—an enormous antique George III partners' desk, Joan's grand piano, and a set of rare carved and painted wood "bamboo" elbow chairs from the Chippendale workshop. The upholstered pieces were covered in a bright English chintz of yellow flowers with deep coral swags and bows on a polished white background. It was an eclectic, welcoming room that could easily seat thirty people.

The rusticated library changed the mood: it had the feeling of a converted room in a barn. The ceiling, walls, and bookcases were made out of old, weathered timbers. Most of the overstuffed furniture was covered in a rather strange Scottish lavender wool tartan; lavender was one of Joan's favorite colors, and the senator also loved it. The wolfskin rug had a story and a short life. When I went to the workroom to help place the skins, I saw similar bullet holes in the backs of the pelts and realized with horror that the wolves had been shot from above, possibly even machine-gunned from a plane. The finished rug looked perfect, but when I told the Kennedys my doubts, the rug was quickly replaced by an American hooked rug. The painting on the massive fieldstone chimney breast was an interesting and amusing Kennedy piece dating from the early nineteenth century. It depicted Irish immigrant navvies working in gangs to build the new streets of Boston. The dining room was more conventional, but it was enlivened by two large canvas screens formed of sets of the French wallpaper company Zuber's early-nineteenth-century series "The Port of New York."

Old timbers and rough stone in the library. The early-nineteenth-century painting on the chimney depicts Irish immigrants constructing the streets of Boston.

The installation took longer than usual—four of us worked at it for a week. When the house was completed, Ted and Joan were in Europe; the senator's secretary said she would warn us three hours before their plane touched down at Washington National Airport. Everything was in place: servants close by, books on shelves, clothes in closets, dinner ready for the oven. Once the call came through, we turned on every light, lit every fire, and drove away at top speed. I said to Tom, "Oh, God! What if the house burns down before they see it?"

Fortunately, that would not be the case. The house was successful and well-used. Jackie Kennedy, when she first suggested I take on the job, told me, "This is not just one project. This is for life." And so it has proved. Over the years, we have helped the Sargent Shrivers, the Stephen Smiths, and the late Mrs. Onassis. Tom Fleming still does work for Ambassador Jean Smith and Pat Lawford. And I would decorate a Boston apartment for Joan Kennedy after her divorce.

Back Bay Apartment

After Joan and Edward Kennedy separated and finally divorced, in 1982, Joan retreated to Boston. Reserved and a bit retiring, she cherishes her privacy and much prefers the calm, mannered anonymity of Massachusetts to the media hurly-burly of New York and Washington. Joan is a seriously accomplished pianist who has played with the Boston Symphony Orchestra; she is also deeply involved in cultural life and in the community of this great old port city. By now, it is forty years since Joan Kennedy and I first met, and for forty years I have admired her spirit, charm, and consideration; *and* she always listens.

Joan had inherited from the Kennedys a big old Back Bay apartment that had been used for political "boiler-room" meetings, a hangout left over from the early 1960s. It had been stripped of its original trim and traditional details and converted into a dreadful, dated open plan. It was awash in plastic and Lucite furniture; ankle-deep, kelly green, geometric shag carpeting; and silver wallpaper.

With architects James Crissman and Peter Seeger, we worked out a revised plan and restored the kind of detail the apartment must have had when it started

The new entrance hall with azure ceilings and bottle green walls. A laurel wreath in one arch encloses Joan Kennedy's monogram.

out in life. The end result was delightfully in character and custom-fitted to Joan Kennedy's wishes, a graceful, triumphant reversal.

The new entry hall was a dramatic enfilade leading all the way to the far living room and almost to the Charles River beyond. Their view always included a sailboat bobbing about—"usually one of my kids," Joan would add. The hall had overscaled cornices; azure coved, groined ceilings; and dark bottle green walls. Matching prettily painted American chandeliers hung from two tiny round-domed ceiling breaks. Every door in the hall and the interconnecting passages was of mirrored glass panels; these produced liveliness in the windowless part of the apartment. The moldings—ceiling, crown, architrave, and base—were vibrantly striped in black, white, and Venetian red. I call this effective old trick my Gucci striping. In one arched break in the hall was a painted laurel wreath with Joan's monogram—my tribute to one of my stars.

The living room at the end of the hall was delicate and muted with pale wheat-colored glazed walls and a beautifully refined Scottish pine mantel, a pair of unusual painted and stenciled Federal elbow chairs, and of course, a tiny injection of lavender on one chair; all shimmered above an old Oushak rug worn close to extinction—the way I like them. The room was an appropriate foil for Joan's good early American furniture. Dreamy and contemplative, it is perfect for Mrs. Kennedy.

Like the living room, the adjoining library had stupendous river views. Instead of doors, we created a screen of faux-pine columns and pilasters so that the two rooms would flow together for large groups. We played the faux pine against hunter green lacquered walls; a practical, bright emerald green sisal rug lightened the room. It was almost, I must admit, identical in color to the 1960s shag carpet! Green linen-velvet and the bold-striped print La Portugaise—in its linen version, which has a more masculine feel than chintz—upholstered the comfy furniture. As Joan Kennedy had three children living a stone's throw away, she insisted on rougher wood tables and chests in the library for a more casual, "feet-up" feeling—the type of room where people could loll about. The oil painting over the large sofa portrays an English sailing ship, the *Ludlow,* in 1836.

Mrs. Kennedy's bedroom was a nostalgic, feminine retreat with walls and curtains in a tiny French stripe and nosegay print. The vast canopy bed was smothered in white Scottish lace. Light-hearted American furniture and part of a collection of nineteenth-century American silhouettes enhanced the room. One of the most interesting design aspects was a fireplace and flue that are shared with the living room; both have similar antique pine mantels. One fire sparkled in both rooms. (I am fascinated by the oddities possible with fireplaces—such as having a fireplace under a window. We did this in a house in London: flues were diverted around the window and came together again above it. The final luxury is an operating fireplace in the bathroom. Admittedly, you need a lot of domestic help to pull this one off. I have managed to sell the idea only once—in California.)

I worked on the job with my late assistant, the sweet Paul Arnold. Joansey and Paul were both blond and beautiful—a smashing couple with whom to share a quick lunch at the Ritz! At the end of a photo shoot after the apartment was finished, Joan suddenly ran round the reception rooms picking up all the cushions and throwing them on the biggest sofa. To Peter Vitale, the photographer, she said, "Now, this is for *me!* This is how Keith would like every sofa, so for me, please take a shot of me and Keith in Keith's idea of heaven." Tableau!

Two domes in the hall with matching chandeliers.

43

Opposite:
A Scottish pine mantel in the living room is surmounted by a fine carved-wood and gilded Chippendale mirror. On the mantel are two outstanding feldspar urns.

In a corner of the library are an eighteenth-century New Hampshire ladderback chair and a lamp made out of a tole Chinese tea caddy.

Scioness in Her Lairs

WENDY VANDERBILT, sculptor and scion of one of the fabled nineteenth-century American families, is a quick-as-a-whip, raven-haired beauty. In the 1960s, she was associated with whiz kids like Mica Ertegun and Chessy Rayner in a group *Women's Wear Daily*—pre-*W*—dubbed "the Locomotives." She was the model for the mannequins in Saks Fifth Avenue's windows. Dressed like a dream, Wendy was much seen in Palm Beach on George Hamilton's tanned arm. Like Wendy herself, her sculpture, for which she retains her married name, Wendy Lehman, is bold, provocative, and certainly not for the weak.

Wendy's father was Alfred Gwynne Vanderbilt, a swell American gent through and through. I helped to decorate his last house, on Long Island, and he was my all-time favorite male client. Wendy met me just after marrying Orin Lehman, the affluent son of Governor Herbert H. Lehman of New York; one observer quipped that it was more a merger than a marriage.

My first few projects for Wendy and Orin were in a big stone town house on East Sixty-fifth Street in Manhattan. It had been Orin's house before he and Wendy were married, and it had been decorated by Ellen McCluskey, Orin's well-known decorator sister. Before I came on the scene—recommended to Wendy by one of her stepmothers, Jean Harvey Vanderbilt—Wendy had tried to assert her own preferences in a couple of rooms with some help from Jansen and Vincent Fourcade. The

Opposite:
Pale blue and white panels in the staircase and entrance hall at Quaker Hill contrast with a rich brown carpet designed by Billy Baldwin.

Bold yellow curtains play off against French printed wallpaper and upholstery in the living room.

spaces, however, remained impersonal with grand but unfinished edges. But before we started on these problems, the winds of change blew two new projects into their married life: a big Fifth Avenue apartment and a lovely old American country house.

Quaker Hill, New York

Wendy and Orin's country house was in Quaker Hill in Dutchess County, New York. The estate had belonged to the journalist Edward R. Murrow, and the interior of the house was far from dazzling—ghastly *dull* good taste. Wendy had considered Billy Baldwin for the country house, but he could not start right away—and help was needed immediately, because Wendy had one young child and another on the way. She considered Carlos Ortis Cabrera of Jansen, but they did not get along. Vincent Fourcade, she felt, would be too grand. Wendy heard that Chippy and I had a year-old daughter, Emma, and lived not too far from Quaker Hill, and that clinched the deal. That was in 1971. Like Wendy and Orin, we had another daughter, Jassy, in 1973. Wendy told me, "I always seem to be pregnant when I hit the next new house project." So in a roundabout way, it was the children who brought us together. Wendy wanted something pretty and feminine but with a down-to-earth, childproof approach.

We decided to use a lot of vibrant, related colors against sunshiny English chintzes. The entry hall was simple and traditional: walls were paneled and painted off-white and deep and pale blue. There was a Billy Baldwin brown carpet runner on the grand staircase and old Oriental rugs on the polished wood floors below. Pretty pots of geraniums marched up the stairs in the summer months, like the steps at Marie-Antoinette's Hameau at Versailles. One side of the entry hall led to a large drawing room and then to a sunroom; the other side led to a library and connected dining room.

The living room was completely lined in an Indienne-inspired, multicolored, French-printed wallpaper with a pale pink background. Most of the overstuffed furniture was covered in a matching French chintz. I have learned, over the years, to use matching fabric and wallpaper in rooms that lack architectural distinction.

Opposite:
In the library, a dark oak French provincial mantel sits against glazed mulberry walls.

48

The dining room is characterized by antique timber trim. Strong ikat-inspired printed curtains tie in with the bold geometric rug.

The one piece not so covered was a monumental Knole sofa—pure 1920s. Like many other sofas, it was adapted from the famous Jacobean sofa still surviving at the great house of Knole, one of the oldest examples of upholstery in England. Wendy and Orin's version had come from a Lehman estate on Long Island; it was certainly vast enough to balance the 1920s portrait of old Mrs. Lehman (Governor Lehman's wife, Orin's mother) painted in *le style Ballet Russe* that hung above. Simple yellow ottoman curtains (a ribbed fabric with a subtle sheen) subdued the patterned walls, and the whole ensemble sat on a grass-green sisal rug—an innovation in those days, and not as ubiquitously de rigueur as sisal is today.

The library opposite had a more masculine atmosphere: dark mulberry lacquer-glazed walls reverberated against whimsical French cotton curtains with a print of fantastical pink and green animals on an ink-blue background. Most of the furniture was covered in the same print or in dark burgundy velvet, and all floated on a softly patterned Irish linen rug (the same kind I had used in Jackie Kennedy's New York dining room).

Salvaged old wood timbers changed the mood in the dining room beyond. Rustic and casual, it was designed to work with Orin's collection of early pewter and his great eighteenth-century Yorkshire oak chairs. The ceiling was planked and beamed; smaller beams outlined the rough-plastered walls. With a bold Kurdish rug on the floor, curtains in an ikat print, and a white-painted French door leading to the rolling meadows of the farm estate, it was a completely bogus banker's Jacobean and thoroughly at odds with the rest of the house—but it was a happy and effective room that suited Orin to a T.

In the sunroom, sponged green trellis work enhances the soft green Rope Lattice chintz upholstery.

On the other side of the house, beyond the drawing room, was an entrancing and cozy folly of a sunroom with trellised pilasters, frieze, and crown and a progression of arches around the walls. All the trelliswork was glazed in pale apple green to marry with Colefax's Rope Lattice. Masses of chintz-upholstered furniture were enhanced by lovely English oak country pieces and rusticated by a thick, woven-reed carpet.

Upstairs were many pretty country bedrooms. The master bedroom was light, with pale sprigged walls. The vast white cotton-draped bed hangings were lined with a mouse-sized pink print; as John Fowler often said, "Your girls *always* look their best in a cloud of soft pink!" Curtains and furniture were mostly in Ribbons and Roses, that eternal English chintz from Lee Jofa.

Silver-ground Chinese paper with ivory foliage covers one wall of the entrance hall. Chippy painted an 1830s-style portrait of the Lehmans' daughter Sage on the velvet cushion on the recamier.

Opposite:
Library with blue glazed paneled walls and blue Irish linen rug.

Family Apartment on Fifth

In the early 1970s, while I was involved with the Quaker Hill house, work was also going on in Wendy and Orin's Fifth Avenue apartment in New York. In a great pre–World War II building overlooking the Metropolitan Museum and Central Park, the apartment was a truly comfortable family home with fifteen or so ample rooms and servants' quarters. It had been built for a style of life that was disappearing. We worked with a wealth of old Lehman and Vanderbilt antiques—in fact, all our projects for Wendy and Orin were linked by such a continuity of personal belongings—and with Orin's impressive collection of nineteenth-century Hudson River School paintings; no surprise that the interior design was deeply traditional but with lively elements appropriate to a home with young

children. (Susan Lehman, Orin's daughter by a previous marriage, was often there, so the atmosphere was brightened by all three smart young girls.)

The large entrance hall was enlivened mostly by hand-painted Chinese Brighton Pavilion—style paper on one long wall. The design was replicated in every direction on the mirrored-glass panels of the other walls. Crown molding, door architraves, and baseboards, stipple-glazed and lacquered in various dark coffee browns, provided accents. The hall had three sets of double doors: to the living room, library, and dining room. These doors were painted deep ivory to recall the ivory tones of the Chinese panels, and also to brighten the windowless room. The most striking furniture in the hall was a pair of matching right and left Regency recamiers found at Eleanor Merril's; we covered them in blue-and-rose-striped satin.

A William and Mary tortoiseshell mirror over a glazed mantel with Blind Earl china.

View of the dining room from the library. Red-lacquered stiles and rails surround the mirrored panels.

The library was a light and happy room. Its robin's egg blue bookcases and paneled walls were stipple-glazed (a blunt stippling brush created an allover pointillist effect rather than an up-and-down strié effect), wiped with a rag for a whitish line at the edges, and finally given a darker stripe to add depth of shadow; thus the paintwork featured three separate subtle tones. This technique—glazing, wiping, and striping—is how we emulate the look of antique painted French boiseries. The walls were complemented by a beautiful faded Irish linen carpet of blue and stone white. We used a spirited old English hand-blocked chintz of pink and red roses on a bright Chinese yellow background for the curtains and most

Two different tables provide seating in the dining room.

of the overstuffed furniture. Dark green linen-velvet and green-patterned fabrics played off against the rich wood and lacquer.

The dining room posed a different challenge. Its one large window faced west, so during the day the room felt gloomy. At gloaming, it was saved by the setting sun, which soon sunk behind the glittering silhouette of Central Park West. We transformed the inferior wood paneling, from the 1930s, by lacquering the trim, stiles, and rails in eight coats of a striking Chinese red; all the large center panels received mirrors of clear silvered glass. Thus the room picked up extra light at midday, and at night the skyline and the romantic sparkle of candles were reflected all around the room. A heavy woven sisal rug relaxed the drama and served as a cool foil for the dark oak antique English furniture, including two

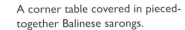

A corner table covered in pieced-
together Balinese sarongs.

A seventeenth-century English Palladian mirror and a carved Chippendale hall table. Towering over an arrangement of Blind Earl plates, Meissen swans, chinoiserie pagodas, and jade Buddhas is a carved-wood and iron nineteenth-century fairground horse.

tables: a parquet-topped table for ten toward the window and an L-shaped banquette with a round table for eight, skirted in a multi-colored Balinese batik, opposite.

Haute Bohemian Duplex

When Orin and Wendy parted ways, Wendy bought an unusual apartment in a Manhattan building designed as artists' studios by Charles Platt in 1906. Over the years, it has been home to many well-known people in the arts, such as Cornelia Otis Skinner, Anita Loos, Marie-Helene de Rothschild, and Harold Clurman. The defining feature of the apartment was a vast double-storied room with overscaled, north-facing windows; the rest of the spaces were in a duplex arrangement.

Wendy was faced with a plethora of "olde Vanderbilt" antiques and *objets* that no longer gibed with her modern artist's mind-set. Together we decided that her new bachelorette setting should have elements that might have been found in the intellectual and artistic circles of Paris between the two world wars—the sort of smart Parisian-style atelier that Jean Cocteau, Madeleine Castaing, Pavel Tchelitchew, or André Gide could have wandered through.

On the lower floor of the duplex section was a tiny entrance hall, an old-world gem leading into the moderne two-story living room. The hall was lined with dark emerald green wallpaper, a jaunty foil for the good furniture, some of it Georgian, inherited from the Vanderbilt family. There were also some eye-catching gilded Italian chairs, dating from the Napoleonic era in Italy, that came from Alfred Gwynne Vanderbilt's house in Oyster Bay. On the console table was a "tablescape"—the word invented by David Hicks—of pagodas and precious porcelain. Above was a sculptural piece that was once part of a nineteenth-century rocking horse: the horse-racing connection was rather powerful in the Vanderbilt family. Wendy and I were great competitors at tablescapes. Wendy once said, "I don't change things much, but in the big room, because of its height, and because the objects are small, every now and then I take everything off every table and rearrange it. I like 'sight' jokes—placing animals or paintings so that they relate to each other in some wry kind of way."

Green, diagonally patterned wallpaper with a subtle border blends with ocelot carpeting in the entry. The carpet design was copied from a 1920s rug Elsie de Wolfe had found in France; she herself copied it for her famous Villa Trianon. The early-nineteenth-century Italian chairs came from Alfred Gwynne Vanderbilt's Oyster Bay house.

The dining room, also on the lower level, was more traditional Vanderbilt fare: glazed apricot walls, outlined with a dashing English wallpaper border with a Chinese puzzle design, and glazed bookcases. One amusing touch was the George II gilt gesso looking glass hanging from an overtheatrical bow atop a larger plain mirror; the whole reflected the antique Chinese painted paper panels opposite. These same panels had adorned the entrance hall of Wendy and Orin's Fifth Avenue apartment. (I always hang antique Chinese papers and European scenic papers over muslin so that they can be taken down easily to salvage their value, or to be made up as screens, or to be used in a different house, as they were here.)

The reflection in the convex mirror hints at the height of the living room.

Two dining tables, each a custom-made lacquered square proportioned for two people on each side, handled both small and large groups. On one side, the tables were pushed up to a Fortuny fabric–covered banquette, and on the other three sides were seventeenth-century oak Jacobean chairs—*very* heavy—from an old Lehman estate on Long Island. These chairs proved to be an unexpected and successful part of this theatrical room—especially as I love to buck trends—because at the turn of the twenty-first century there is nothing more out of fashion in *le monde* of desirable antiques than real Jacobean chairs. In fact, they have been politely *out* since the early 1920s—but they sure work well here!

To carry the scale of the spectacular living room/studio, we commissioned Harrison Howard III, an artist from California, to faux-paint the walls with large stone blocks. He also painted a distressed carved-stone dado and pilasters. A trompe l'oeil carved keystone on one architrave featured Wendy's monogram with the Vanderbilt family oak leaves. I copied the moderne-looking crown molding, a pyramid-stepped cornice, from a 1930s example I had seen at the Musée d'Art Moderne in Paris. The bars on the panes of the Mondrianesque window and the overscaled black-framed Van Eyckian convex mirror over the simple bolection molded mantel echoed the early-twentieth-century feel of the space. It is very right for today. Every successful room I see has an element of black, and as Sir Edwin Lutyens, the great early-twentieth-century English architect said, "Every room should have a line of black in it."

On the ceiling were overlaid blocks of silver-leaf paper, their glossy sheen reminiscent of the *hôtel* Jean-Michel Frank decorated for Marie-Laure de Noailles

Opposite:
A trio of Wendy's wood sculptures stands near the bar. *The Night Visitors* was based on the Three Wise Men.

One of a pair of vast black-lacquered bookcases on either side of the fireplace. A wide opening leads into the dining room.

Opposite:
Seventeenth-century Jacobean carved-oak chairs are used in the dining room. The banquette under the George II gilt gesso mirror is covered in a Fortuny fabric.

in Paris. On the floor was a sisal rug, its supersized coarse texture and wide, bold black border quite startling. It had been custom-made in Guatemala, woven to stretch from wall to wall . . . and it fitted perfectly, thank *le bon Dieu!* The living room was built to be flooded with light, which suited the scale and boldness of Wendy's collection of modern art and her own pieces of sculpture, as well as the scattering of inherited Vanderbilt furniture. The biggest of these pieces were covered in Le Lac chintz, always one of Irvine & Fleming's favorites, especially here where the large repeat of the design works so well with the room's proportions. (The design originated with an eighteenth-century French chinoiserie brocaded silk by Philippe de la Salle, who designed brocaded silk textiles for Marie-Antoinette's bedroom at Versailles. Le Lac was adapted into a fabric print in the twentieth century.)

The large two-story space proved to be perfect for entertaining—it could accommodate anything from an intimate group to a large crowd. High in one of the walls was a black-edged window that opened from Wendy's second-floor bedroom, and other parts of the walls in rooms above had been cut out to overlook the living room. From the main level, upper-floor observers peering down from these apertures recalled the airy, peopled perspectives of Tiepolo in the Palazzo Labia in Venice.

The apartment, which included a drop-in bedroom and bathroom for Wendy and Orin's now grown-up daughters, had an erudite and unmistakable haute bohemian edge—and a large quota of glamour, as befitted its artist owner. More Wendy than me—the way it should be—the interior was dashingly bold, though screened by my well-honed eye. "People who come here like it," says Wendy. "They find it festive." 🐾

Media Empress in Manhattan

ONCE DESCRIBED as the most powerful woman since Queen Victoria, the late Katharine Graham was *the* superstar media mogul of the latter part of the twentieth century. After the death of her husband, the gifted Philip Graham, she was catapulted into on-the-job training and proved to be an inspired leader of the family businesses—the *Washington Post, Newsweek,* and their many subsidiaries.

A naturally shy woman with an endearing, occasionally almost awkward manner, Mrs. Graham had an admirable habit of keeping silent until she was sure of her ground. She first approached me on the recommendation of two of Washington's reigning social arbiters, Mrs. Averell (Marie) Harriman and Mrs. John Sherman Cooper. I had already completed Georgetown houses for both of these women. Nevertheless, Marie Harriman warned, "Do everything Keith suggests, but okay only half the number of cushions he proposes."

I first worked for Mrs. Graham (I never called her Kay) on her vast R Street house in Georgetown in about 1962. She was hesitant about what she wanted—but she knew it was *not* the grandeur for which her overbearing mother, Mrs. Eugene Meyer, was famous. In fact, Mrs. Graham had never worked with a decorator before. Many years later, in Nantucket, I bumped into Stephen Graham, her youngest son. He explained to his friends, "Keith was the first person to work on my mother's houses. Before that it was all Sears, Roebuck!" This meant that all the work I did for Mrs. Graham was under tight budgetary constraints.

After the Georgetown house, I worked on a charming eighteenth-century farmhouse near Front Royal, Virginia. During a weekend visit, I mentioned my close friend Chippy so many times that Mrs. Graham finally retorted, "Why don't you marry the girl!" Long before we actually *got* married, when the whole team

A desk, leather-covered tub chair, and brass and glass bookcases à la Billy Baldwin in the library.

Opposite:
Dominating the living room in the apartment is a painting by Adolph Gottlieb. The white cotton damask upholstery on the sofa matches the walls and curtains. In the foreground is an English Regency saddle-shaped bench.

One scarlet cushion leads the way in a sea of dark English linen print.

was finally installing the farm, Chippy came down to help. I suggested she unpack the books and arrange them on the bookcases throughout the house. A fashion designer then, she decided to organize the books by color: in Mrs. Graham's pretty blue and white bedroom, I suddenly discovered every shade of blue-dustcovered book she owned.

Shortly afterward, Mrs. Graham bought a river-view apartment in the then newly built United Nations Plaza. Her apartment, like most in the building, was laid out on an open plan (except for the bedrooms and bathrooms), so we developed a flowing tonal background that was rich but timeless in feeling. We swept a white-on-white polished cotton damask around and through the interlocking spaces: walls, curtains, and upholstery. The living room area was spiced mostly with Meyer family antiques, including a Coromandel screen and some Chinese landscape paintings, but was enlivened by Mrs. Graham's growing collection of American abstract paintings by artists such as Adolph Gottlieb, Kenneth Noland, and Frank Stella. All this sat on a spirited blue and white geometrically patterned broadloom carpet by David Hicks—the first patterned broadloom carpet I ever used. The carpet became so popular that it was copied and commercially produced. When I visited the apartment some time later, all the building's corridors were carpeted in the same design—it appeared as if they all led to Mrs. Graham's apartment. Both she and I were vastly amused.

The library was the complete opposite of the other areas: it was atmospherically dark with a dramatic edge. The curtains and walls were hung with a hand-blocked English linen print of vibrant aquamarine and off-whites on a rich chocolate ground, which imitated a Jacobean crewel design of flowers and vines. The bookcases—an homage to Billy Baldwin—were copies of the steel and brass ones he had so famously designed for Cole Porter. They glittered against the somber, dusky background color.

In addition to the bookshelves, black-lacquer cupboards with doors held Mrs. Graham's papers. She worked at a large round table skirted in scarlet Roman dull-faced satin. Sitting at the table were some tufted Georgian side chairs covered in black leather and a pretty black-lacquer elbow chair that she herself used. The rest of the furniture in the room was covered in the Jacobean-inspired print of the wall hangings and curtains. One of the prettiest elements in the room was a pair of fine oval Irish Regency Waterford mirrors: they echoed into infinity across the space.

After Mrs. Graham had been using the apartment for a time, the late Greg Jordan came to Irvine & Fleming. Greg could execute anything physically—he even, willingly, took our two young daughters to a rock concert! He recalls, "My first brush with Keith was at the impressionable age of twenty-four— I was working as his assistant. That seemed to serve everyone, as I could install a crystal chandelier, then crawl off the ladder, wash my hands, take off my tool belt, and tie grosgrain ribbons

A round, skirted table with English Regency elbow chairs and a black leather tufted Hogarth chair in the library. Mrs. Graham used this table in the nineteenth-century manner, for conversation, reading, writing, and the occasional solitary meal.

on pictures on the wall. My first day, Keith sent me to Katharine Graham's apartment at U.N. Plaza, which needed an uplift. I was scared to death, but he gave me a couple of tips and said, 'Bring me back a scheme.' I think most of what I got right was by accident—a kelly green table skirt to go with the blue and white geometric rug, beige upholstery, and white wallpaper flecked with little black thistles."

Much later, Mrs. Graham wandered away from our advice—one of my greatest disappointments. Her life on the world stage forced her to present a more fashionable appearance, and she began working with other decorators such as Parish-Hadley and Nancy Pierrepont. Later, one of Mrs. Graham's great chums told me that she had been advised by her friends that Irvine & Fleming was neither grand nor expensive enough. Because we had tried so hard to keep within a lean—sensible—budget, and because I admired Mrs. Graham so much, it was a lesson both sad and somewhat ironic. 🐾

A serene hall opens onto colorful
rooms that relate to each other.

Park Avenue Perfection

JON AND SUSAN ROTENSTREICH are an attractive couple originally from Alabama and now living in New York. I worked with them on a country house in Bedford, New York, and a ranch in Wyoming before starting work on their duplex, in one of architect Rosario Candela's most prized Park Avenue apartment buildings, in 1986. My then assistant, Sam Blount, was himself from Jackson, Mississippi. I have always had a penchant for southern charms and sensibilities—I love to recall that Prime Minister Henry Palmerston kept the news of the American Civil War from Queen Victoria for over two months (she was in hibernation up at Balmoral) for, as she was to state, she would certainly have brought in England on the side of the South!

A painted Sheraton elbow chair with a beautiful paneled mahogany door behind.

Susan, a jewelry designer, has a great eye, a sense of style, and a passion for the decorative arts; she always understood the romantic appeal of English taste. Early in her marriage, she had worked with Mario Buatta—once my assistant—so she was well-versed in the Anglo angle of pretty bows and doggie paintings. She had a commendable collection of unusual eighteenth- and early-nineteenth-century English pieces—so much so that two decades earlier the Rotenstreichs would have been irresistibly drawn to John Fowler!

When Susan and I first met, Susan has told Chippy, "We were feeling each other out, but we soon found each other simpatico. Keith's attitude resonated from an artistic and an intellectual standpoint. He had a vision and could see the picture of a room in his mind." The concept for the apartment was to create the comfortable and lived-in yet stylish feel of a grand London town house—but in a New York apartment building. We were working at a time when everyone in the United States thought they could do the English country house look. Across the nation were rooms rampant with "a ghastly sea of ruffles," as I said, and "packs of Staffordshire dogs," as Chippy said. In reality, anyone who knows English country houses knows they have precious little comfort to offer.

Opposite:
Cranberry-glazed walls set off a Scottish bleached pine mantel in the library.

Following pages:
The voluptuously comfortable drawing room mixes patterns and colors with riotous abandon. The fine antiques and a meticulous attention to detail hold the assemblage in check.

The master bedroom is a tonal composition with walls, curtains, and sofa covered in a Venetian-design *toile de Jouy* on linen. Pepper, my favorite cat on all of Park Avenue, knew he enhanced the room.

The floor of the entry hall was laid with real stone in muted hues, the various tones pulled together by dapper black diamonds. Paneled mahogany doors led to a series of rooms in related colors: a piquant apple-green-lacquered dining room; a shimmering daffodil-yellow-glazed drawing room; and a deep-cranberry-stipple-glazed library. Each room, like the entry floor, had a stroke of Lutyensesque black for emphasis. In the library, it was black frames on architectural engravings, black-painted Regency chairs, and black trimming on an easy chair and ottoman; in the dining room, a black line on the dado and black ribbons tying striped slipcovers onto chairs; in the drawing room, an exemplary antique

Regency needlepoint rug with flower motifs—no two alike—on a black ground. The drawing room was eclectic, its English country jumped up to a smart urban level by blue and white silk festoon curtains and my beloved English chintz Trenton Hall (still a major favorite of Irvine & Fleming; see pages 149 and 211.)

The master bedroom upstairs told two stories. Susan had enjoyed a colorful feminine bedroom with a mix of classic ribbon- and rose-patterned chintzes— remember, mixing chintzes was a top game in the 1980s—for fifteen years, but she was also feeling a change in her design thoughts. We used the same pieces of furniture but created an all-over, tonal room. The main fabric was a beige and sepia Venetian-patterned toile de Jouy–style print on linen. It looked as though it was drawn in the 1920s, for though inspired by the finely drawn copperplate prints of the eighteenth and nineteenth centuries, it had been sketched by a freer hand and printed on a more textured cloth—the effect was completely different. This fabric wrapped the walls, became the curtains, and covered some of the furniture *en suite* (as the French say). Simple beige and brown checks and stripes covered the rest of the pieces. On the floor was a tonal beige wool carpet that imitated the unpretentious look of sisal but was softer to bare feet. The refurbished room was more reflective, a lovely lesson in how a single space may be transformed with the wave of a wand.

The apartment has endured well; the owners insist that, like fine wine, it gets better all the time. Walls have not been repainted in twenty-five years, and still they look as good today as they did then. "Things that are well executed last a long time," says Susan. "Keith encouraged us to make some extravagant purchases, something I've never regretted."

Highly detailed traditional projects like this need years of accumulation of *objets d'art* and pictures to bring the decoration to life. Clients either have to trust the designer, providing an almost carte blanche budget, or must do it for themselves. In Jon and Susan's case, my job was simplified because the art and antiques were very personal, and mostly purchased by the couple. When the apartment was featured in *House & Garden,* Jon Rotenstreich said, "We know a lot of people who are into major glitz, but we're trying to de-glitz." Anyone who remembers that era will recall the emphasis on flamboyance. My own thought was that these rooms would one day look pure 1986—and would become yet another style to be imitated.

Anglophiles in America

Wʜᴇɴ Mɪᴄʜᴀᴇʟ Nᴏᴄʜ and I first met in the wild 1980s, he was back in New York after spending a lot of time in London. He had moved in cosmopolitan circles, and he was partial to the comfortable ambience of an English home where everything looked as if it had been pulled together from two or three previous residences. I was inspired to find that Michael was, like me, an avid reader of history and the classics. Every third book in his library was about ancient Greece and Rome. These traits would come into play not only in New York but in Florida and Nantucket once Michael had married and started a family.

London Transplant

Michael had just bought a beautiful apartment in a prewar building on Fifth Avenue; its windows looked across to all those snapping banners outside the Metropolitan Museum of Art. A serious Anglophile, he was considering several of my major competitors, and he had almost been seduced by Denning & Fourcade when he interviewed Irvine & Fleming. "I walked into that drawing room they had when the office was on Fifty-seventh street," says Michael, "and I thought, I want this room! I think before that I had been preparing for the time when I could afford someone of Keith's caliber."

The interior of the apartment had just been beautifully redone by the previous owners, decorative fabric and wallpaper entrepreneur Eldo Netto and his late wife. We kept some of these elements but most of it was structurally re-formed and redecorated to suit Michael's taste. (Luckily the kitchen stayed intact—how I hate kitchens!) After some preliminary discussions at our office, I took Michael to see

Opposite:
The hall walls are hung with hand-painted Chinese paper. Faux-bamboo painted Regency chairs flank a serpentine-fronted Hepplewhite hall table.

Michael Noch's Chinese wedding chest before the panels of a three-fold mirror.

some antiques. By the third stop of the afternoon, he was restless. "Look, Keith," he said, "I don't have the time to scoot around like this. I'm going to go with anything you think is right." Gosh! I felt like Fowler, or even Elsie de Wolfe! My late assistant, Paul Arnold, and I shopped in London and New York for almost every piece of furniture and all the pictures and porcelain in the apartment. During our year of work, Michael never once visited. He told me afterward that he would occasionally sit on the steps of the Metropolitan Museum, gazing up at the apartment windows and pondering our progress.

A brief digression: I have to say that it is easier to work with a guy. Once men feel real confidence and trust, they restrict you far less than any woman. With couples, on the other hand, the wife always seems hampered by some undefinable cage

An eighteenth-century secretary desk stands against the far wall. A table to the right holds a bust of a young girl by Houdon; on the walls are early-eighteenth-century engravings of great English houses. The coffee table has a lacquered-straw finish.

of guilt. I think that many wives feel they should be able to put a house together for their husbands, and maybe save a little money. But there are always exceptions, and I certainly have female clients who are open to taking a chance!

The large and welcoming entry hall was enlivened by faux pine on the trim and doors. The walls were wrapped in hand-painted Chinese garden foliage wallpaper panels. The one piece of furniture that Paul and I did not buy—a Chinese wedding chest Michael Noch had bought in London—stood in the hall.

In the drawing room, we left intact the Nettos' yellow-glazed walls. A room properly prepared, painted, and overglazed can last for more than three decades—but it should be professionally washed every five or six years. When I suggested that we preserve the yellow glazing, Michael, so nice and bright, said,

In the dining room, *faux-bois* architectural detailing surrounds a grisaille scenic wallpaper depicting the story of Cupid and Psyche. Neoclassical plates sit on an eighteenth-century English sideboard.

"Can you imagine any American agreeing *not* to let you repaint the walls?!" We did wash them, of course, and we added a fillet of powder blue wallpaper all around the room—top, bottom, corners—to bump up the vibrance a couple of notches. The room was a perfect "ten" of instant accumulation, a lived-in, eclectic whirl featuring an English carved-pine mantel, a Russian square pedestal table, a painted antique Hepplewhite elbow chair, a black-lacquer Regency fire bench, and an exemplary George IV gilt and ebony bull's-eye mirror (installed on a plain modern mirror, a well-seasoned device of ours). We used a sunny Cowtan & Tout English chintz for curtains and most overstuffed furniture.

Another digression: Mrs. Cowtan and Mr. Tout had been brought to America by J. P. Morgan to import British fabrics just for him, and they knew or cared

Chintz-covered chairs and Regency-style curtains in the dining room.

little about self-promotion. Few New York decorators were familiar with their wonderful English chintzes. Many years ago, the pair, aging and sharing an almost Dickensian office in New York, had tried to persuade Irvine & Fleming to buy the firm. Instead, ten years later, it was Eldo Netto who would step in. And today, well-known and successful, Cowtan & Tout belongs to Colefax & Fowler.

The dining room was lush and formal, a neoclassical dream of faux pine columns, pilasters, and cornices with elaborate Regency-style, asymmetrical, heavy satin curtains. The tour de force was an antique grisaille Dufour scenic paper—scenes of Cupid and Psyche—that we found at Gracie & Sons in New York. The scenic panels had probably papered some Parisian house in the nine-teenth century; we had them restored and bordered with a black and gold Greek key. The room was spiked with a two-tone blue antique Serapi rug, a blue dado, and high-backed dining chairs upholstered in a lively Fortuny chintz. The mood was pure 1840—a candy apple for Michael and me.

The library was diminutive and received almost no daylight, but it was rich with atmosphere—the room of a perfect London gent. Walls were lined with splendid mahogany paneling that had once adorned an eighteenth-century London shop; the set included a handsome broken pediment that married the mantel flawlessly, leaving a horizontal space ideal for a Japanese watercolor of an early steamship. Soft furniture was covered in a luxuriant plum, pink, and aqua English striped chintz from Lee Jofa. Alas, it is no longer available, though I used it—probably overused it—for thirty-five years. A svelte George II wing chair in its original leather sat beside the fireplace on my favorite Elsie de Wolfe ocelot-patterned wool carpeting. The room was sturdy, yet so tiny it recalled the famous library in Queen Mary's doll house at Windsor Castle, famously designed by Sir Edwin Lutyens.

Leading into the master bedroom was a thickly padded, studded green baize door. I have designed similar doors, my personal indication of soundproof privacy, for several clients, starting with Vivien Leigh in England. One of my long-time favorites, the La Portugaise brown-striped floral linen print, provided a masculine edge. This fabric used to be an exclusive with Rose Cumming, the charmingly eccentric decorator and *antiquaire*. I first saw the design in her great, crazy Park Avenue shop—an Aladdin's cave of beautiful and ugly (she *loved* ugly!) *objets*. Rose, garbed in printed-organdy garden-party dress (her ample bosom softly spilling out) and vast, floppy picture hat, casually put me down for fourteen yards. As I left the shop, she reached for the telephone and called my office: "Rose Cumming. Mr. Irvine was here, and you owe me $338, and I'd like a check before lunch!" Perhaps she needed it to pay *for* lunch. *Quel* style! The fabric, still a favorite, is now sold by Brunschwig & Fils. The bedroom furnishings rested on a Wilton patterned carpet called Garbo. Evidently, Greta Garbo had owned the antique Bessarabian rug from which the Wilton carpet was devised.

When the apartment was almost complete, a friend of Michael Noch's asked

Opposite:
The La Portugaise linen-print curtains in the master bedroom have a heavy natural linen fringe. The padded baize door is an element I have used many times to signal privacy.

Paul Arnold, "Well, what does it look like?" Paul quickly answered, "Just like Keith—with money!" It was a lovely and satisfying job for us all—perhaps most for our bachelor client.

Nantucket High

Michael Noch returned to Irvine & Fleming a number of years later. By then he was married to Regina; they had three adorable sons and were living in Naples, Florida, where the lifestyle was more relaxed. The Nochs gave up the Fifth Avenue apartment when they moved, taking some of the antiques and selling others. (Jacqueline Kennedy Onassis bought the Japanese watercolor that had been in the library.)

Michael and Regina had always loved Nantucket, vacationing there regularly with their sons. Then, in the mid-1990s, they got the opportunity to buy one of the island's most distinguished houses, East Brick on Main Street. This house was one of three "great old ladies," as they were called, that had been built between 1836 and 1838 by whale-oil merchant and shipowner Joseph Starbuck for his sons, George, Matthew, and William. Our objective was to suggest the home of an earlier, well-traveled merchant family without sacrificing any of today's creature comforts. The Nochs' wondrous cache of really good antique furniture—mostly purchased by Paul Arnold and me for Michael's apartment—was a not insubstantial resource.

The entrance hall, like most of the house restored but not drastically altered, was brightened by a wallpaper of scattered, predominantly green (with touches of coral) motifs and widely spaced stripes on a light ground. An ivory and coral needlepoint rug perked up the polished wood floor. A red-patterned wool runner edged with Chinese fret borders sat atop the gracefully curved staircase leading to the second floor.

Off the entrance hall was the north parlor. We lined it in sunny two-tone yellow stripes, which provided a great foil for the Nochs' collection of engravings of English country houses by Johannes Kip. A simple border subtly fenced in the stripes, and strong yellow bands highlighted the white-painted crown molding. On the ceiling was yet another paper, this one with fine gold stars on a white ground. The upholstered pieces of furniture were covered in Le Rosier, a

This "tablescape" includes a neoclassical bronze, a Staffordshire antelope and pitcher, and a Sevres saucer.

Opposite:
The American Empire settee in the entrance hall is covered in American Independence toile, which was originally manufactured for the American market after the Revolution. The La Nancy wallpaper is an early-nineteenth-century French documentary design.

The four-poster bed together with its hangings and the window curtains remain from the previous owner.

Cowtan & Tout print of wide, sky blue and white stripes smothered with overblown roses. The windows, which looked onto the street, had white Scottish lace curtains.

As in many nineteenth-century houses, a second parlor (in this case, to the south) was separated from the first by a pocket door. For the wallpaper in the south parlor, we selected another two-tone yellow stripe, but in stronger shades. Two windows that had been blocked by a 1970s-era addition at the back of the house were disguised with an infill of mirrored glass and Scottish lace curtains (different from those of the north parlor). From inside, especially at night, our little deception effectively resembled real windows. The room was furnished with a mélange of

Opposite:
The entrance hall opens into the north parlor with its custom-made two-tone wallpaper and its custom-made chandelier from Charles J. Winston & Co.

Noch antiques; a dramatic black-lacquered Coromandel screen almost completely covered one wall. The American crystal chandelier in the north parlor has a few red drops; the one in the south, a few green drops. "I love color, and Keith's at his best with his sense of color," says Michael. "We talk the same language. I can finish some of his sentences, and he can always finish mine."

On the other side of the entrance hall was the library. Its more masculine mode—leather-covered chairs and a calfskin-covered bench in front of a black marble fireplace original to the house—was a complete contrast to the parlors. The walls were covered in spruce green strié wallpaper from Brunschwig; the ceiling paper repeated the tiny stars of the parlors but on a green ground. The wood trim, including paneled shutters behind curtains of Cowtan & Tout's Bailey Rose, was painted green with lighter highlights. On the floor, a needlepoint rug called Fontainebleau picked up the color of the polished floorboards with its brown ground. Bookshelves were finished with gold-tooled, green leather edging.

Lending a dreamy effect to the dining room were sepia-painted canvas panels of Nantucket Harbor created by the artists at Gracie & Sons from nineteenth-century prints. Interspersed mirrored panels added to the floating, watery atmosphere. Shadow painting, both light and dark, finished the panel surrounds and crown molding, and the ceiling, once again, was dotted with tiny stars. Clustered on the sideboards was a collection of rare early Spode and Herculaneum plates—how they caught the eye! A Fortuny chintz that slipcovered the dining chairs picked up the colors of the plates.

The project included not only restoration but alteration to the addition tacked on to the back of the house by the previous owners. The proficient space planning of my former partner, Jason Bell, would transform this add-on. Jason was a graduate of the University of Alabama. On his first job-hunting foray to New York, he was offered positions by four design firms; he chose us and became my assistant. Jason was immensely practical at installations, showed a gift for space planning, and absorbed the best elements of traditional and modern design concepts. In April 2004, he left to form his own company.

Jason made over the addition as a child-friendly yet aesthetically pleasing family room. White-painted columns bestow a sense of style, which is played down

Vieux Paris porcelain urns, from about 1820, and a nineteenth-century bronze copy of a Greek bust on the mantel in the north parlor.

Opposite:
The black marble mantel in the north parlor—like that in the library—is original to the house. The nineteenth-century American Empire settee was found at the Little Shop at Macy's, which used to have very nice antiques. Other antiques included a Roman bust on a pine column and a George III painted and gilded elbow chair.

Sepia-painted panels depicting a harbor scene are interspersed with panels of mirrored glass in the dining room. The table is set with eighteenth-century Canton plates, which match the blue sleeve of the Gothic-style lantern.

by striped-denim-covered furniture, white cotton rugs, ceiling fans, and a simple pine table surrounded by Windsor chairs. "The furniture gets moved by the boys," says Michael, "but it stands up to them and the classic look is still there."

The Noch family's East Brick reflects the sensibilities of Nantucket, both past and present. It recalls the bustling, if short-lived, whale-oil boom in its size and

quality and also in the played-down luxury of its furnishings. Nautical motifs mate-
rialize at every turn: on the grandfather clock in the hall, in a Japanese watercolor
in the library, on the evocative panels in the dining room. So the phantom presence
of the nineteenth-century Starbuck family remains, but as a family that has enjoyed
the refined delights of London.

An Irvine Half-Century

BEFORE CHIPPY and I got married, I was living "over the shop" and Chippy had a small, dark apartment within walking distance of her job in the garment jungle. It was her place, far from ideal, where we started life together in Manhattan. We soon found another, rather undistinguished apartment nearer my work, but it proved to be too small once we started thinking of a family so we moved to a quiet street in Murray Hill and into a pretty walk-up brownstone, which was decorated in a simple, basic way. We and our two daughters lived there until 1975, when our congenial landlords decided to sell it.

Chippy always walked to work, and as she walked, she would check out the various apartment buildings en route. By chance, she stopped to talk to the superintendent of a building just opposite the Pierpont Morgan Library. He was thrilled to hear about our two children—he had children of about the same age. I really think we got the apartment—still our Manhattan domicile—only because the children could all be companions. And they are still friends.

Murray Hill: The Blue Period

The apartment is in a sturdy building originally erected for workers at the Morgan Library (Chippy's father's favorite New York museum) in Murray Hill. It has a view past the spire of the Church of the Incarnation at Thirty-fifth Street and Madison Avenue, overlooking an open courtyard behind the church, and toward downtown Manhattan. When the previous owners discovered that Chippy and I were British, they said, "Oh, you will just love it! When we light the fire in the evening and look out of the living room window, we imagine we are in Grosvenor Square."

Opposite:
The upholstered furniture in our Manhattan living room is covered in loosely fitted beige-and white ticking slipcovers. Sir Roy Strong noted in an article in the *London Times* that the stack of unread books beside my chair could become a moveable telephone table or a drinks tray.

Already installed when we moved in was a rather mediocre mantel. It has been faux-stone glazed and surmounted by a Scottish pine mirror. The fireplace is flanked by two Edwardian chairs covered in blue Hollyhock chintz.

That was a *bit* of a stretch. But we decided the mood should be light, easy—and child-friendly. We hung the walls with sky blue strié wallpaper, which set off slightly stronger blue chintz curtains. A cultivated mix of furniture, pictures, and objects came partly from our family homes in England; the rest we acquired over time. Our upholstered furniture was casually slipcovered in beige and white mattress ticking, and we covered some odd pieces in the great old blue-background Althea English chintz. Cotton slipcovers (or loose covers, we called them in England) can be easily laundered and also add a homemade edge I love to see creep into almost any room. Everything floated on a lovely, soft blue and white Irish linen rug. The composition was influenced by my favorite literary subject—descriptions of English houses in books, such as those in volumes by Vita Sackville-West and Francis Brett Young—yet also alluded to my own experiences at that point in my life.

I have always loved arranging and endlessly rearranging rooms. Tom Fleming and I have had deep satisfaction out of generating a new ambience from existing elements. For the U.S. Naval Academy in Annapolis and the American Embassy in Oslo, Norway, we created two completely dazzling transformations with *nothing* new—thus doing ourselves out of possibly lucrative jobs—but oh, the satisfaction!

Our living room in the apartment reflected this enjoyment. A stack of still-to-be-read books stacked beside "Dad's" chair and ottoman was used as a movable drinks table; the volumes also hinted at the increasing value of time and reflected how I tried to keep my mind vibrant and adaptable. Our daughters were never intimidated or limited by the presence of antiques and fine objects, and over the years, the only serious casualties were an exemplary Battersea box, which our dog Victoria ate, leaving only the copper rim of the lid and a sprinkling of enamel, and a large, antique silvered witch ball, which the cats knocked into smithereens.

Many of the personal mix of ingredients have moved on: the bust of Prince Albert, consort of Queen Victoria, as a Roman general is now in the hall of St. Johns Farm; two overstuffed Edwardian fireside chairs went to live with Mrs. William F. Buckley Jr.; the leopard-print-chintz slipper chair with a cigarette hole (left from the days when we all smoked) now resides elsewhere in New York City.

The long passage of the kitchen included a breakfast area. Around a circular butcher-block table were four bentwood chairs lacquered in red, blue, green, and yellow. Chippy still maintains that this was not such a great idea: there was endless contention over who got what color, and no one was ever satisfied with yellow. The chairs, now painted black, are in constant use in our country kitchen.

The little bedroom, once shared by our daughters, then reworked as a guestroom, was, as Chester Jones wrote in his book *Colefax & Fowler,* "a very pretty bedroom . . . The layering of pattern and detail, to which many found and treasured possessions are then added, is typical of Keith Irvine's work. This romantic approach is finally more concerned with the overall mood than with any individual item in the decoration." The walls were papered in an innocuous allover print; horizontal and vertical bands of wallpaper border gave the effect of decorative paneling. The curtains and dust ruffle were made from a Colefax two-flower print.

The master bedroom was romantic and old-fashioned—a safe haven from the tumult of Manhattan. Three walls papered in the great "Fuchsia Arch" pattern from Leixlip Castle were echoed endlessly in the fourth, mirrored wall. Our bed was garnished with an old American Star of Bethlehem quilt and had a half-canopy of white cotton *broderie anglaise*. Next to the bed was Nancy Lancaster's painted Regency kneehole desk from Haseley Court—we used it as a bedside table. It is now a little drinks bar, used the way Mrs. Lancaster did it, and is very much at home in our ballroom at St. Johns Farm. Above the desk was my favorite John Vere Brown photograph of Chippy in 1960s Italian movie star mode.

A black-finished plaster bust of Queen Victoria's consort, Prince Albert, as a Roman general with gilded armor surveys the living room.

Murray Hill: Red at Night

A decade or so after our "blue period," we heard rumors that some houses nearby—one a respectable-looking, old-fashioned shop that sold Rudolf Steiner books and tracts—were to be pulled down. There were some local attempts by the Murray Hill Association to save the buildings, but the demolition went ahead and our light and views vanished abruptly as a new sliver building quickly went up. I was even more aggravated when I discovered that one of my most admired clients had provided the seed money for the project!

In a corner of the living room is an English Regency mahogany and maple slant-top desk with a Louis XVI mirror above. The Louis XV *bergère* desk chair was covered in a now extinct red, blue, and white version of the print Verrières. On the wall is a grouping of early-nineteenth-century German watercolors of birds decorated with real feathers.

Beside the bed is a painted Regency kneehole desk that belonged to Nancy Lancaster. We used it as a night table.

Because I am an early-to-the-office and late-to-home workaholic, we decided to transform the suddenly gloomy apartment into a snappier, more urbane night-time setting. Living room walls were treated to eight coats of lipstick red lacquer, windows to stylishly draped and smocked curtains of matching red linen with self-ruffled leading edges. This intense color dialed up the drama of all our family antiques, paintings, and objects. Accents were provided by elements of black

running through the room: wallpaper borders, picture frames, and pieces of furniture. One of the most potent pieces was a distinctive William IV tufted lounge chair of the type so beloved by Englishmen. This chair was covered in a much-used French toile in red and white, "Dame du Lac," which illustrates Sir Walter Scott's epic poem *The Lady of the Lake* (see page 192). A ravishing French Empire Savonnerie rug soothed the vivid room. It was so expensive that I called it my Porsche, but it seriously augmented the glamour.

This iteration of the living room had an eclectic mix that reflected my decades in decorating. It gradually acquired a host of personal intellectual games that summed up the essence of my life in *le monde du décor*. Most personal of all was the worn, decorated, black Hepplewhite elbow chair sitting at the coffee table with its back to the fireplace. This painted Regency chair was and is one of my most-loved antiques—everything that turns me on. I bought it in Paris many years ago from that grand *maman*-of-us-all, Madeleine Castaing. On one visit to her beguiling antique shop on rue Jacob, when she was well into her ninth decade, I had selected some pieces I wanted to buy. *La grande madame* was advised of my wishes, and I was bid to call at six that evening for an answer and an aperitif. When my assistant, Sam Blount, and I returned, we found Madame in full *maquillage* and ready to receive. She sported a stylish wig on her ninety-year-old head, a dashing pair of fitted jodhpurs, and a resplendent scarlet jacket. All in all, she was *quelque chose formidable*.

She spoke almost no English, so for over an hour I travailed with my school-boy French. We progressed through impressions of other decorators—mostly denigrated by us both—and of our famous clients, including Jackie Kennedy. Years before, in a moment of exasperation, I had advised Jackie to consult Madame Castaing. Jackie, always supremely independent, had listened assiduously to Madame's drops of wisdom—but in the end took none of the advice.

At the end of our cocktail hour, Madame arose from her Hepplewhite elbow chair and gestured to it: "Celui-ci, c'est pour vous, Monsieur, mais celui-ci seulement. Pas les autres!" In our endless rearranging, the chair Madeleine Castaing sat in was moved from our New York apartment to our country ballroom, where it floats serene and happy.

The living room is reflected in a convex mirror and re-reflected in the mirrored panel opposite. A Landseer-like portrait of a dog hangs on the panel.

Opposite:
Our red-at-night transformation retains the faux-stone mantel in the living room, but replaces the Scottish pine mirror with an oversized English convex mirror of about 1810 and flanking gesso and gilt triple swan sconces. Dotted around is a collection of silhouettes and miniature portraits, and in the foreground is my beloved Madeleine Castaing chair.

Desire under the Maples

Chippy and I had lived in Manhattan for about six years when we both felt the urge to put down some roots in the New World. Chippy was feeling footloose, and I ached for a country retreat away from our New York apartment, where I could relax on the weekends. We had seen a perfect property in Connecticut, but we dithered for a couple of hours and it was sold from under our noses. We would not make that mistake again.

We looked at a map and drew a seventy-mile radius around New York City. A hamlet called Sodom caught our eyes. Chippy envisaged hilarious invitations ("Do come to Sodom for the weekend"), but when we set out in my little red Triumph, we found only a reservoir and a real estate dealer who insisted that all the houses he showed us were old—"Yeah, least ten, twenny years old!" Though he was soon fed up with us, he took us along a dirt road to a ramshackle clapboard farmhouse where the setting April sun was glancing on daffodils under the trees. It was Desire under the Maples. We were not quite married yet, and so we each gave him a check. In fact, we were so naive that we did not realize we were supposed to offer less than the asking amount.

St. Johns Farm when we found it— a small core from 1830, with a larger wing of 1876.

St. Johns Farm from the air, nestled in its woods.

After the closing, we returned to our property. We found squirrels' nests in the two attics, grass growing through the rotting kitchen floor, leaks everywhere, and a host of broken windows. There had never been any electricity, and the well was long since dry. It had belonged to only one family, the St. Johns (in England, it would have been pronounced "Sinjun" in that exasperating British way), and no one had lived there for a quarter of a century. The property had a wonderful view of Harlem Valley cattle farms and the Connecticut hills and had become a favorite horse trail and picnic ground. For the first months, we had to wash in local lakes, entertain by candlelight on packing cases, and sleep on mattresses on the floor. We thought, vainly, that we would have the whole place put to rights by Christmas.

Two years later, when we married, the library (of course) was the only civilized room. We completed the library in anticipation of a visit from Chippy's parents. We had to have one room where the Reverend and Mrs. Grime could escape from the packing-crate chaos of the rest of the house—and also from all our *talkative* friends. We even put a skull-and-crossbones "Private" sign on the door. Curtains and upholstery of English linen in the Hare & Hounds print sat against crisp tartan wallpaper and lots of white-painted, blue-lined bookcases.

Dubbed by us the "Tudor room," this original part of the house once included a larder. It was used both as a living and dining room. We painted the rough plaster walls white and rescued two ceiling beams from our old barns. The fireplace replaces a window. The skirted table sits up to a Jacobean oak settle/table/chest. The screen depicts grisaille "Portraits of English Monarchs" by Zuber. Over the beam mantel is a portrait of me as Mary Queen of Scots by the Mississippi artist William Richards and a carved-wood Austrian stag's head with real antlers.

On one wall in the sitting room a good Adam oval mirror is flanked by two portraits of horses. The frame armchair came from Chippy's father's family in Lancashire, where it was always called the "courting chair." Chippy slipcovered it in a brown toile called Jockey Club.

Chippy made the shaped valances, which hung from nineteenth-century *faux bois* and gilt cornice boards—these were among the few things in the house when we bought it. Hare & Hounds, which combined a repeat of two dogs with garlands of plump pink roses and morning glories, was one of my favorites, but it was discontinued in the 1970s because so many people objected to the dead hare under the sitting hound's paw. The fabric company redesigned the print without the hare, but they lost all the subtlety of the original and I have never used it since. On the center bookcase hung a pastel portrait of a girl by Christine Andrews—a society portraitist of Newport, Rhode Island, in the 1920s. I had discovered several of her pastels in a Newport thrift shop, including one of nineteen-year-old Myrna Loy, a socialite before she began to act. To the right of a walnut slant-top desk was a stage throne made of painted wood and papier-mâché patched up with duct tape; it had been used by Vivien Leigh in the film version of George Bernard Shaw's play *Caesar and Cleopatra*.

The dining room (or "Tudor room") was in the oldest part of the house, a low-ceilinged room built in the 1830s. It had rough (and collapsing) plaster walls, old beams, and our idiosyncratic mix of English oak furniture. Our first piece of serious furniture was an Elizabethan chip chest—so called because there was a similar one in the Victoria and Albert Museum in London. It was an ingenious early convertible and could be used as a bench, storage chest, or table. Now it belongs to my partner, Tom Fleming. It is likely that our dining room was once an all-purpose living room; it was even smaller when we found the house because part of it was walled off, perhaps serving as a larder. There was also a root cellar,

104

which is now hidden under a carpet. There was no fireplace, so we installed one; nearby was a chimney for a Franklin stove, which would have been the latest thing in modern convenience when the modest farmhouse was built.

The Hollyhock-print curtains were just as English as our oak furniture. I had already used this hand-blocked, red-ground print many times for my clients. The cotton tablecloth, a paisley design printed with a batik technique, was one of the myriad I had made for Jackie Kennedy; it had been rejected and returned. Immensely practical because of its color and pattern, we still love it and use it almost fifty years later.

Among the varied pictures we hung in the dining room was a portrait of a brown terrier, Binks, which had belonged to Chippy's grandfather. It was painted in 1914 by an itinerant pet painter called—coincidentally—Mr. Binks. Chippy's grandfather trained dogs to do tricks and sold postcards of them to raise money for the R.S.P.C.A., all while running an antique shop.

The library with tartan wallpaper made in Germany.

Irvine & Fleming was reticent to go public in those days—we agonized as to whether it would help or hurt the firm. But we did photograph the house, for *House Beautiful*, with its Christmas decorations and for other publications as well. The holiday shoot took place on one of the hottest days in August, and between the lights and heat, the candy canes on the tree melted. Nevertheless, our beloved cat Macavity (pre–*Cats* the musical) made the December cover of the magazine.

The drawing room (today our main kitchen) was a soft, sunshiny room worked around the English hand-blocked Orchid chintz with walls hung in coral red strié wallpaper (one of the first times I used this now ubiquitous strié paper).

House Beautiful cover shot.

A very "me" plethora of objects arranged—and endlessly rearranged—on a table in the library. The leather-covered chair with brass nail heads is Irish. The photograph of the nurse is my mother in France during World War I.

Everything sat on a patterned sisal carpet. An inlaid William and Mary burl walnut cabinet and a Chippendale mirror above came from Chippy's family. I bought a marble bust on a pedestal, which we dubbed Hermione, though she is a copy of the Medici Venus in the Pitti Palace, from a fascinating Suffolk *antiquaire* fifty-six years ago. Her name escapes me, but her shop was memorably called Impecunious but Aesthetic. In 1947, Hermione cost all of two pounds!

The guest bedroom was not large, and it was almost all eaten up by a bright Chinese red lacquered canopy bed. I love overscaled furniture in small spaces—

A carved and ebonized wood-framed mirror in the Egyptian style over an Italian bombé burl walnut desk. In the corner, blocking an unused door is a piece of movie furniture found in a thrift shop—the throne used by Vivien Leigh in *Caesar and Cleopatra.*

it doubles a room's assets. In this case, the bed became a room in itself. It was draped in an antique blue chintz from Eleanor Merril, and the tiny sprigged lining was made from the same material as the sheets and pillowcases. On the old chestnut floor was a worn English needlepoint rug. The peachy leaf-design wallpaper was one I had ordered from France a year before for the Connecticut house of Felicia and Leonard Bernstein. First, I guessed at how many rolls the Bernsteins might need for their bedroom; then Felicia double-checked with her local painter, who added more "just in case"; then Felicia herself added "to be

A watercolor of the guest bedroom by the late Mark Hampton.

sure," since it was hand-printed and coming from Europe; and finally, Irvine & Fleming jumped the number up once again because it was an import. So crates of paper arrived—enough for the inside *and* outside of the whole Bernstein house—and the Irvines and the Bernsteins ended up with matching bedroom walls. (Felicia also gave scads of rolls to other Connecticut friends.) Mark Hampton's watercolor of the room, from his book *Mark Hampton on Decorating* (he nicely gave me the original one Christmas), romanticized it further—and he cleverly summed up his feelings about this room, and my work in general, in his book: "A guest bedroom in the farmhouse of Keith and Chippy Irvine demonstrates many of the advantages and possibilities of smallness. Mr. Irvine's exuberant gift for whimsy is widely known and when coupled with his notable tendency to avoid stuffiness, it often results in rooms that possess tremendous comfort and spontaneity." Groups of pictures could be glimpsed from the interior of the bed. On one wall was an early-nineteenth-century mahogany hanging shelf cluttered with blue and white china—some of it eighteenth-century Chinese but most of it Staffordshire with scenes of American beauty spots and buildings.

In the master bedroom was an even more massive Lincolnesque bed, a castoff from one of my earliest clients, Mrs. Frances Leggett (see page 201). Her son Lord Margesson was born in it. On the headboard we inserted a watercolor portrait of my great-grandfather as a boy. The wallpaper came from an American firm, Jones & Erwin, set designers on *Gone with the Wind*. The dark chintz curtains depicted a variation on the theme—birds, fruit baskets, and garlands.

The scarlet-lacquer poster bed is hung with a late Victorian printed chintz from Eleanor Merril. The mouse-sized floral print lining matches the bed linens. The rug is an English antique floral needlepoint.

We called the tiny blue and white guest room the Marie Antoinette room, not to ape hotels grand or kitschy but as a running joke engendered by me and my cohorts at Colefax & Fowler in the 1950s. We had an ongoing fantasy that John Fowler was really a reincarnation of the hapless queen. This was tenuously based on our observation that he entered doors sideways, as if he were managing his panniers. My friend from boarding school, London antique dealer Stephen Long, also had a thing about Marie-Antoinette. So when Stephen came to stay, we did up the guest room in homage to the French queen, right down to invented "last letters" from the *conciergerie,* pricked out with a pin. The room was full of (mostly concocted but heartfelt) Marie-Antoinette mementos on a background of French

The view through the hangings of the guest bed. The arrangement of decorative pictures ranges from a "sailor's valentine" made from shells to a Regency tinted engraving of a little girl entitled "Daddy's Darling."

sprigged wallpaper. The nineteenth-century Gothic-inspired Hudson River bookcase came from Eleanor Merril; the painted canvas *paravent* (a screen, literally "against the wind"), my first purchase from Colefax & Fowler when I worked there (it cost eight pounds in 1956). The blue and white French print Verrières, probably the pattern Irvine & Fleming used for the longest time, was a three-color batik-style design created by the Swiss designer Jacques de Luze in 1810 and printed in France by the venerable fabric firm Le Manarch. The design was most famously used by poet, artist, and muse Louise de Vilmorin at her family's Château de Verrières: in the early 1950s, she covered every piece of furniture in the large drawing room in this fabric, which was then called Batik. Some members of her family were famous seedsmen, and *verrières* means "greenhouse"; this is the name used by Brunschwig & Fils, the firm licensed to sell the fabric outside France.

Our daughters' nursery bedroom was an illusion of little-girl childhood based to a large extent on the illustrations of Henriette Willebeek Le Mair. The lace-edged dotted Swiss bed hangings were attached to cup hooks on the ceiling with simple, baby blue picot-edged ribbon bows; it was easy to take them down for laundering. The nineteenth-century maple sleigh bed beneath—complete with wood slats—was donated by a friend. This much played-in room, awash with dolls and bricks, micro men and matchbox cars, was instant infant clutter. As I say, "Get 'em used to it early."

By the time the children came along, Chippy and I had spent twenty years in and out of each other's company. We had developed a stimulating, bantering rapport, topping each other's anecdotes and dovetailing our domestic duties. We were both vastly amused when the journalist Stephen Drucker described us (and our décor) as "Mapp and Lucia meets Colefax & Fowler" in an article in *House & Garden* in July 1993.

The Marie-Antoinette bedroom has a tiny sprigged wallpaper; all the pictures had some connection to the French queen. The castellated American Hudson River bookcase came from Eleanor Merril.

A flagstone path that we have bordered with plants—and with varieties of thyme between the cracks—led to the cottage. We did—and still do—all our own gardening except for mowing the lawns. The "Gothick" window was a birthday present to me in 1967.

Garden Cottage

Over the years at St. Johns Farm, we tamed land enough for walkways, apple trees, herbaceous border, fenced-in vegetable garden, statues, herb beds, grape arbor, two fountains, faux-crumbling-stone tower folly, and simple stone-edged, rectangular, grass-surrounded, hedged-in swimming pool. Even the garage looks kinda romantic! The property originally included two barns, several multiseated outhouses, and a laborers' cottage, but in the early days, we were forced to pull down the great old timber barns. They were in perilous condition, and we did not have the money to save them. We did keep the superb old hand-hewn chestnut beams and soon put them to use as we transformed the laborers' cottage into a pool house.

We built a new foundation for the eight-room clapboard structure, and one week, while we were in the city, it was moved from a back driveway to its new position. Once the cottage was firmly in place, we gutted the interior, exposing its post-and-beam structure. We worked with a creative local contracting family. Every weekend, we would look it over and discuss the next step. We added many of the larger beams from the demolished barns to enhance the exposed interior skeleton; others formed an exterior portico for wisteria, silverlace vine, and climbing roses.

The theme print in this two-story room is a design of tulips on the tomato ground by Suzanne Fontan. A white vinyl-covered armchair is a practical idea for any pool house. Above the chair is a bucolic painting of me, Chippy, cat Mavis, and dog Victoria by William Richards.

The main room became a large, two-story space, fine for entertaining fifty people and equally fine for work projects or the children's playtime. To one side we installed a simple rough-beamed staircase with bookshelves fitted underneath; the stair led up to a sleeping balcony, where we used beautiful, original nineteenth-century chestnut planks for flooring. Underneath this sleeping balcony and overlooking the main room, we fitted in a small kitchen leading to a screened-in porch and a hallway leading to a bathroom.

There were many different types of wood—some lovely, some less so—in the now exposed construction, and so we had the whole interior spray-painted white. Some observers criticized the painting of the magnificent chestnut beams (we did the same in Ted and Joan Kennedy's house in Virginia; see page 39), but we were after a light, summery beach-house look; perhaps I was envious of Tom Fleming's neat, simple house in the Hamptons. Chippy was never that fond of beaches— "sand in everything, no escape from the dreaded sun"—so there was to be no house in Southampton for us. She also assured me that the magic of Tom's neat-as-a-pin house could be achieved only in a childless, petless situation. So we instead inflected the interior decoration toward America–cum–south of France.

Because it was in part a pool house, and because it was the 1960s, we put in a white, nonskid tile floor, easy to walk on and to clean, which was indestructible for parties and even for our two young daughters. We added a lot of white-painted vintage wicker furniture, a bright Moroccan palace rug, and comfortable stuffed furniture slipcovered in a multicolored, tomato-ground French cotton print by the legendary Suzanne Fontan, probably designed sometime in the 1940s. I had first spied the fabric in a magazine showing a Long Island house designed by Billy Baldwin, and I bought some in Paris as an homage to him—I still consider him the best American decorator. The tulips in the print were echoed by wall sconces and by a rusty iron chandelier with white porcelain tulip fixtures.

One area of the big room was set aside as a dining area, though as a rule we tended to eat on the porch. Around an oval table, faux-marbled by myself, was a set of white-lacquered chairs with backs of interlocking ovals; yellow vinyl seat pads were practical for wet swimsuits. The chairs were adapted from an eighteenth-century Portuguese set once owned by Ronald and Marietta Tree.

The kitchen has a blue and white nonskid tile floor, blue and white Treilliage wallpaper, with counters and splash walls of rustic Portuguese tiles. A door leads to the screened-in porch.

Opposite:
On the fireplace wall is an arrangement of farm implements we had collected. A Moroccan palace rug lies on the floor.

The fully exposed, white-painted framing in the cottage. The eighteenth-century New Hampshire high chair has survived many children, including our two; it has a practical design with a woven locust seat. Teddy, Emma's constant companion as a child, was a gift from my late sister, Willis. The nearby ladder was constructed so that we could reach the skylight.

Within the sleeping balcony was a queen-sized box bed that could be rolled out from a wall recess under the eaves; the recess was formed by timber-disguised closets on either side. Chippy made the quilted bed coverlet from a Louis XIV chinoiserie design printed on linen; the same design backed with paper covered the interior walls and sloping eave. Again the choice was an homage: this design had been used by John Fowler in his weekend getaway, King Henry's Hunting Lodge, in England.

We partitioned from the sleeping loft a small private bedroom for our children—there was just enough room for twin beds. We gave them proper framed Beatrix Potter prints when they were small (and we still had some control over the décor), but by the time they were twelve and ten, they had covered the walls with lurid posters of rock bands and hand-drawn, life-size pencil drawings of legs with ballet slippers.

A screened-in porch was added on to the cottage in the early 1970s. The floor was easy-to-hose-out flagstone. White-painted wicker furniture was softened with cushions of a French fern print. Vintage metal Parisian park chairs were used around the dining table for casual meals.

In both kitchen and bathroom, we emphasized the beams by painting the spaces between them bright blue and tomato red. The work space and walls of the kitchen were lined with hand-painted Portuguese tiles that depicted fruits, grains, vegetables, fish, and farm animals. Mealtimes for the girls became lessons in recognizing and naming the produce on each tile.

The screened-in porch was successful as both a casual dining room and an almost-outdoor sitting room. Plants hung in baskets from the rough ceiling beams or were arranged on vintage white-painted wire stands. It was a lovely place to have a drink in the evening and watch the moon reflected in the pool; no matter how hot it was, a soft, cool breeze constantly whispered through. Furniture was mostly white-painted wicker with cushions in a great green and white fern-printed French cotton Elsie de Wolfe had commissioned for the sunroom at her beloved Villa Trianon in France. These cushion covers are almost forty now; they are being nurtured into longevity by a careful hand-laundering and -patching at the end of every summer.

The cottage became such a happy little house, so much more than just a pool house. We moved there lock, stock, and barrel every year from late May through early October—a vacation house only a hundred yards from our vacation house.

Ballroom Rêve

Toward the end of the 1980s, I was suffering a late midlife crisis, part of which was boredom with St. Johns Farm. This was perhaps triggered by Tom Fleming: he had already had five houses (more were to come!), while we had only the one. I felt restricted by the small rooms in our Victorian farmhouse, and I longed for spaces with real architectural merit, in particular one that was vast and slightly grand. As Emma's graduation took place in a simple yet expansive Greek Revival church in Massachusetts, it burst upon me that *that* was the scale and ambience of the room I craved.

The north facade of our new ballroom wing, looking romantically Russian in the snow.

At first, I thought of selling the farm and looking for a more stylish house, perhaps in Connecticut (shades of *Mr. Blandings*). Chippy was reluctant, our daughters horrified. Besides, anything good was going to be far too costly. So I began to think of adding a new wing that would consist mostly of a great room, and Bob Liebreich, an architect with whom Tom and I had previously worked, and I played about with some ideas. I surged ahead, fired with enthusiasm and ego, but selfishly I did not involve Chippy. Though she spent far more time than I did at St. Johns, we did not include her in any specific plans until the project was well under way. As she commented in Stephen Drucker's 1993 article, "Oh, it was a power thing surely." Once we showed her the model, Chippy sensibly cut the great room's size in half. "Keith's strengths are the formal rooms," she commented (to which she now adds, sotto voce, just don't let him near a kitchen!). "It is probably going to be the most beautiful room in the whole of America."

In the six years it took to build the new wing, Chippy was faced with dirt, dust, and scores of invading workmen. Her office was moved five times. Let this be a warning: it was a point of crisis in our marriage of forty years, almost splitsville. Chippy threatened to do a beautiful drawing of the new wing and engrave it on thick, expensive stationery with the house name Keith's Erection. But humor prevailed, the trauma was surmounted—and the ballroom, everyone agrees, is truly a great room!

Numerous alterations to the farmhouse itself preceded construction of the new wing. We enlarged the house by taking over the original porches, and we

Opposite:
In the entrance hall to the new wing, an antique English pine door leads to a cloakroom with Chinese paneled wallpaper. The French Directoire chandelier is bronze d'oré.

Invitations are tucked into the frame of one of a pair of Italian mirrors that echo each other across the dining room. Flanking the bottom of the mirror are watercolors I did as a student.

replaced two staircases with one. The original kitchen became a guest wing (with a new bathroom), and the girls' bedrooms were revamped. Also re-formed was the library, which became our formal dining room.

When we first lived at St. Johns Farm, the library was the favored refuge of Chippy's parents, the Reverend and Mrs. Grime. Prior to that, the St. John family had used it as a billiards room. We extended the area considerably by building out to include part of an old corridor and part of the front porch of the 1876 wing of the house.

Two architectural screens of white-painted wood columns and pilasters now divide the new dining room into three sections. Centered in the main section was a nineteenth-century expandable mahogany table under an antique Swedish crystal chandelier. The table was surrounded by a mix-match set of antique English and Irish chairs. Italian silver-gilt looking glasses mirrored each other across the table. Below one mirror was a "mechanical" William IV serving table, which rises to form two levels; below the other was a Hepplewhite-style bench with rolled arms upholstered in red-striped glazed chintz. Two large bronze urns on pillars flanked the bench. (In the eighteenth century, these would have been used to rinse wine glasses.)

One of the two smaller sections, formerly the corridor, housed my favorite piece of furniture, a dramatic, almost theatrical cabinet that is, as far as I can tell, by William Kent. It dates from that unusual moment in the early eighteenth century when Palladian classicism was being overtaken by the first stirrings of a romantic, literary English "Gothick" style. I bought the cabinet in the late 1960s from Eleanor Merril. It cost more than the car I drove in those days, and it is still my favorite possession. Set in a mirrored alcove, its quotient value in the room was tremendous.

The dining room table laid with early Wedgwood plates with leaf borders. In the background was a bust of Robespierre, infamous during the French Revolution, next to an antique French landscape screen.

In the smaller section at the other end of the room—once the porch—was another table for small dinners or luncheons, or for extra seating at large dinners. It was often used by our children and their friends, who were happy to be at one remove from the "monstrous regiment" (grown-ups, that is). Along with the round, skirted table (too many legs were showing in the room as it was) were some small-scale *faux-bois* painted American country chairs of the Federal period, which we found in Maine for a hundred dollars each. Nearby was an antique

The section of the dining room near the window holds a circular table suitable for four to six people. Around it are early nineteenth-century American *faux-bois* chairs found in Maine; above the table is an Italian painted and gilded umbrella chandelier made in Florence.

Italian neoclassical marble-topped serving table that had drifted my way from the Agnelli *palazzo* in Turin—or so I was informed by the antique dealer in Nice. Two Russian crystal candelabra atop the table added great glitter to a dinner party. Presiding over this section of the room was a white marble bust of Lord Perceval, the only British prime minister assassinated in the House of Commons.

The walls of each section of the dining room were papered in varying designs. I love wallpapers and always have! There were three different white, gold-star-scattered papers on the ceilings; three papers for the walls, each with appropriate crown molding border; two dado borders; and two simple baseboard borders—thirteen different elements of wallpaper all in one room. Hanging on the walls were pictures, plates, brackets, and sconces. The effect was not confusing; the dining room had the cinematic atmosphere of an English Regency room—but in America.

All the alterations to the house took place in the year before we began construction on the ballroom wing proper. The exterior of the new wing was painted white to accentuate the contrast with the red farmhouse. The front entrance was a Georgian pine-paneled door I bought from Michael Crowther in London, one of the antique dealers I most enjoy seeing. Flanking the door were Edwardian terra-cotta terms in a pillared porch.

The entrance hall appeared simple—but it was certainly *not* something one might expect to find along a country dirt road. The walls were punctuated by pilasters bearing Corinthian capitals inspired by those in one of the anterooms to Catherine the Great's bedroom at Tsarskoye Selo, outside St. Petersburg. It had been designed by Charles Cameron, her imported Scottish neoclassical architect. The Russian originals were faux-marbleized over gold leaf; ours were faux-marbleized, more rustically, over silver

An Italian marble-topped side table, purportedly from an Agnelli estate, and a Regency mirror framed in bleached pine. The antique crystal-drop candelabra are Russian.

leaf. Intersecting these pilasters was a plaster anthemion frieze. Walls were shadow-painted—naturally!—in various tones of gray. This choice was inspired by the Christian Dior shop on the Avenue Montaigne in Paris; the original concept, I would guess, was Emilio Terry's. On the paneled walls hung an exemplary set of watercolors, dated 1735, of British birds by the much-respected Eleazar Albin, all in their original ebony and gilt frames. These were interspersed with a series of unusual antique Liverpool Transfer plates with three-masted man-of-war ships.

Encaustic floor tiles, cleverly copied in London from nineteenth-century prototypes, were set into a dark, polished wood surround. With their black and white Greek key border, they looked old but still dapper. The tiles added a sensory element I have always enjoyed: the sound of shoes walking across a hard floor. The central domed ceiling was painted with passing clouds and supported a stylish French Empire bronze-doré chandelier.

Between this entrance hall and the original farmhouse was a long stepped hall with an open staircase leading to the second floor of the new wing. This hall was carpeted in a two-tone, green and tan, geometric Wilton carpet. The walls and ceiling were hung in a tonal green Brunschwig wallpaper, Fôret Foliage; the effect was romantic and replicated the feeling of passing through a space completely lined with some leafy old tapestry. This greenery was a fitting background for off-white-painted bookcases, trim, and banisters. An antique pine door led to the dining room in the farmhouse.

The staircase itself was carpeted in Elsie de Wolfe's tonal brown ocelot-patterned rug. (Elsie had had it copied from a needlepoint rug she found in Paris in the 1920s.) The sides of the staircase are always piled with still-to-read books. Books are not assigned to bookcases until they are read. Soon it will be time to panic: there is not one foot left in the farmhouse for another bookcase, and Chippy has placed a firm moratorium on any more additions—not even a possibly glorious library in the style of Sir John Soane!

The structural steel posts at the juncture between the ballroom wing and the farmhouse were focal points. Chippy faux-painted them as stylized palm tree trunks, then attached fringed leaves, cut from thin metal and painted, with neatly wound household twine. Anyone who has visited the kitchen of the Royal Pavilion at Brighton will recognize the inspiration.

Opposite:
The wallpaper in the upper staircase was designed by Owen Jones for the Houses of Parliament. The steel engraving showing Pharaoh's daughter finding Moses in the bulrushes, bought in Burford, Oxfordshire, was a birthday present from Chippy to me.

A painted Regency recamier smothered in cushions.

The entrance to the Elsie de Wolfe Memorial Library was an asymmetrical mirrored arch necessitated by the slope of staircase above.

Branching off this long hall was a small, irregular library/sunroom with a low skylighted ceiling. The room was partly the result of a miscalculation, but once built, it was papered in Brunschwig's classic French wallpaper, the green and white Treillage; a matching trellis frieze separates walls from ceiling. On the floor were American Olean tiles in a tricolor Roman receding-square design. Tiles made good sense: it was easy to water the plants we kept here in the winter, and also to mop the floor when we opened the French doors onto the upper garden terrace in the summer. We called this room the Elsie de Wolfe Memorial Library, partly as an homage to the founder (self-described) of our profession, partly because she was the spunkiest pro at a time when women did not speak up or out. When I first came to New York, I met an intriguing old German curtain woman who had worked for Lady Mendl. One of the many fascinating stories she told me about Elsie was her response to over-questioning clients: "Who's doing this job?" she would say. "You or me?" Bravo Elsie! (Actually, the *real* reason the room acquired its name was because it contained four chic 1930s painted-bamboo fret-pattern chairs Lady Mendl had in her last house in Beverly Hills in the 1940s. I bought them from a San Francisco antique dealer in 1986.)

The small room was mostly white-painted bookcases (biographies and history); a nice faded mahogany Hepplewhite breakfast table acted as a reference/ writing table. Also in the room were an eighteenth-century French oak *bergère* and a late-nineteenth-century high-backed garden armchair identical to one in a Monet painting at Giverny. The curtains, on iron spear poles, were a French floral chintz depicting bamboo leaves, and hanging on one wall was an oil painting of

A French bamboo print is used for the curtains and also on a cushion for the Giverny-green-painted garden chair; the lamp base is a Chinese famille rose vase.

the chestnut allée at Hampton Court in the snow by my Kingston Art School friend, the photographer and painter manqué John Vere Brown.

I had my "chambers," as Chippy calls them, upstairs in the new wing: modest bedroom, bathroom, dressing room, and most important, studio. The bedroom was an aerie looking out over the roof with its windowed cupola and "flying pheasant" weather vane. It gave me that solitude of final relaxation. The wallpaper was blue and white "Montgolfier" toile de Jouy; the curtains a blue-gray-silvery

Fortuny cotton. The Directoire bed was blue-painted steel, and the long Provençal rush-seated bench was a catchall for books—as are most things in our house. A decrepit plaster bust of some eighteenth-century worthy on a reeded pillar surveyed me sardonically; he looked positively sinister in the first shafts of morning sun. I found it at actor/antique dealer Tristram Jellinek's London shop. It was my private nod to chapter one of Nancy Mitford's *The Blessing* (read it to catch what I mean!). On the bedside table stood my real 1940s telephone (I hate push-button phones, cell phones, e-mail, voice-mail, et cetera, but I must admit I quite like faxes!)—it was the sort that Joan Crawford could have used as a murder weapon.

When I started putting this room together, I had in my mind that it would be a spare, almost Quaker-simple room with a slim bed and perhaps only three or four other things. I was inspired by my memories of Governor Averell Harriman. The very grand Federal house on N Street in Washington, D.C., that I decorated for him and his wife, Marie, in the early 1960s, was super-fancy and crammed with top-notch Impressionist paintings (now in the National Gallery). Marie Harriman's bedroom was lush, French, romantic (Jackie Kennedy copied it when she moved to New York), but the governor's bedroom was spare, empty, simple. It had a narrow maple bed, narrower even than a twin, possibly from his days at Groton; an enamel-topped metal table; one hard maple Windsor chair; a modest cotton rug—it was the perfect spartan nest for this American eagle.

I envisioned my bedroom as a room in which to meet my God, the place where I would silently die ("the undiscover'd country from whose bourn no traveller returns")—a "dying" room, the opposite of those traditional New England "borning" rooms. Of course, being a room of mine, it gradually got cluttered up. I have never cottoned to "less is more." The more the merrier, say I!

On to the main event. The ballroom was forty feet square and thirty-six feet high, with a chandelier-lit dome and cupola. Four vast, faux-painted, reeded Ionic columns defined the center of the room, dividing it into nine segments. The concept was neoclassical, influenced by our trip to Russia in 1971 and my passion for Swedish Gustavian "country" grandeur. (I rationalized it by imagining that back in the 1830s, a well-to-do landowner on the fringes of our straggling hamlet could have built a temple-style house similar to one of our still existing neighborhood

Opposite:
My bedroom was intended to be sparse, but it has become cluttered—as always. The toile Montgolfier was designed at the height of the ballooning craze in France.

The entrance to the ballroom guarded by Maude, our golden retriever.

churches.) Russian-inspired also were the eight large arched French doors—glassed on one side to overlook the rolling landscape and mirrored on the other side for *Smiles of a Summer Night* dances and *Nutcracker* Christmas parties.

The ballroom wing was built on a slightly sloping hill, so the formal entrance hall with its faux-marbled pilasters and the anteroom (dark brown faux-paneled wallpaper, brown mirrored glass, faux-tortoise-painted closets) led to a pair of outsized, glass-paned doors, rescued from a New York convent. These opened onto a small balcony overlooking the ballroom itself. Next was a divided horseshoe staircase. All told, this enfilade of rooms gave a gala sense of parade, and yes, most people do say "Wow!"

The wood floor of the ballroom, in pure Swedish eighteenth-century style, was faux-painted in faded gray and white in a neoclassical geometric pattern. It was antiqued to look as though two hundred or so years had worn it into contented disrepair. In the central panel, within the four columns, was a stylized circle design depicting some emblems of my life and interests—the Union Jack and Stars and Stripes furled together, architectural drawing implements, a Scottish thistle and an English rose, and a skull (indicating that life is transitory), all circled by a Latin proverb: *Ars longa vita brevis est sed vita longa si scias uti* (roughly, "Art is long and life brief, but you can make life long if you know how to use it").

There was detail piled on detail, none of it sharing an obvious color scheme. The walls, hand-painted in the palest blush strié glaze, were so tall that three specialty painters had to run up and down ladders, handing off the brush so as not to break the vertical sweep. Recesses flanking the fireplace and on the balcony were accentuated by dark-coral-glazed walls.

I originally conceived the room as being minimal. That aspect has long since

View to the ballroom entrance with the glass doors and the double horseshoe stairs. Prominent is a period copy of Mme. Recamier's settee as painted by David but with many more pillows.

passed because I love to arrange assortments of our favorite things—don't we all? On the walls, a lifetime's idiosyncratic collection of paintings, prints, drawings (two tiny ones by my great-great-grandfather John Martin—Queen Victoria's favorite painter), and watercolors (285 at last count) plastered the accessible wall space.

The furnishings were a mix of much-loved antiques arranged into intimate seating groups, along with floating "character chairs" to move with the crowd. John Fowler always said that chairs should "move to talk to other furniture." Most of the pieces had spent previous years in other Irvine rooms. Some were upholstered in one of my favorite Colefax prints in strawberry and cream, Gothic Scroll, and a faded-to-perfection red silk

In the center of the ballroom is a painted cartouche depicting the story of my life. In front of it is my favorite Hepplewhite chair from Madeleine Castaing.

velvet enhanced the huge Mme. Récamier–style David settee. A French oval-backed chair was covered in Brunschwig's naive Moons and Stars design. But most of the overstuffed pieces were slipcovered in small-scale beige and white prints, checks, and stripes. In winter, color is introduced to the room by a mélange of cushions—what the Americans call throw pillows—while in the summer all the chairs are slipcovered in white canvas with the cushions mostly covered in variations of green-printed toile. This is a wonderful way to ring in seasonal changes, and it also protects upholstery from the ravages of sunlight for six months of the year. But be warned, says Chippy, the slipcover material must be preshrunk, or the covers themselves must be *very* loose, because they must be able to stand up to frequent laundering. (Originally, slipcovers were simply plain pieces of inexpensive cloth draped over furniture to keep the dust off the actual upholstery, which was more expensive and faded easily. Thus they were called

Opposite:
In a corner of the ballroom is a black lacquer Coromandel screen with Nancy Lancaster's painted Regency desk in its new role as a bar table. The antiqued and faded painted floor was inspired by the eighteenth-century floor in a Swedish house.

133

dustcovers. Over time, covers were shaped to a particular piece of furniture and called, in England, loose covers, and in the United States, where they were even more fitted, slipcovers.)

Many of the pieces were oversized, to conform to the large scale of the room. We had a "relic" table, inspired by Sir Walter Scott's octagonal relic table—it had knocked Chippy and me out on a visit to Abbotsford. Our table was originally a 1920s display case from Cartier. It takes up a good bit of space, but it also doubles as a buffet table when needed. Its partitions separated our English, Scottish, French, German, Russian, and American mementos. From time to time, we amuse ourselves by inventing fantasy relics of our own—a lot of Sir Walter's relics were bogus too!

Suzanne Slesin wrote of the ballroom in the January 1997 *House & Garden:* "The pavilion—a Russian summer palace springs to mind—with a soaring 36-foot-high dome [is] frothy and grand but also [a] surprisingly cozy great room." The vast columns cry out for crinolines, and the double entry horseshoe staircase was made for glamorous entrances and for weddings—we have had two sparkling ones already—yet I have always felt the ballroom to be, spiritually, a fine place in which to be alone.

Opposite:
An eclectic seating group gathered around a severe Georgian settee found in the French Quarter of New Orleans. One of my favorite painted Louis XVI *bergères* was covered in real old jaguar skin.

This corner of our relics table contains memorabilia of Jacqueline Kennedy, including some amber worry beads she brought me after her first visit to Skorpios, and a black sleeping mask that once belonged to Marilyn Monroe and still shows vestiges of her pancake makeup.

The mood of the room constantly changes through every hour of any sunny day. The light moving through the grand arched French doors, and the beams glancing down from the fenestrated dome, contribute to an ever-changing yet tranquil illumination. (Certainly our cats recognize this as they move to each new patch of sunlight.)

Mostly, it is a space that epitomizes a lifetime of thoughts and passions about life and houses. I have always been drawn to the notion of played-down grandeur. This idea was instilled during the Fowler years, though mostly jump-started by the dauntless Nancy Lancaster. She played with great architecture, great furniture, and great paintings as if her latest project was a theatrical fantasy—but she did it with originality and consummate assurance. I learned from her that nothing in a house should ever be set or static. She advocated constant rearrangement—chairs on the march, pictures endlessly rehung. And never bother about the old nail holes—they are just the age spots of a fully lived life!

These two, John Fowler and Nancy Lancaster, produced in me a fierce desire not just to create pretty rooms designed around the latest charming print but to assemble a setting against an architectural background with a mix of comfortable things that look as if they had drifted in. They might seem to be family odds and ends or things of no serious importance—almost wrong or even an edge ugly—and often give the impression of having been used elsewhere. Typical of this is the favorite Louis XVI *bergère* that I covered in old jaguar skin; I reused the French brass nails, which had weathered to an elegant verdigris. The animal skin, the French decoration, and the nail heads decaying from the Caribbean salt air: I fantasized that the chair had belonged perhaps to the Duchess of Windsor and might have come from Government House in Nassau when the Duke was governor general in the 1940s.

I have called this look "instant accumulation," but it is more an idiosyncratic psychological scene that mirrors the passing years. There should be a feeling of things that do not quite go together—fabrics that look used and have nothing to do with the overall scheme. Though it may appear accidental, all is deliberate. It is the layering of life as it happens.

Our ballroom was, and is, a mirror held to my soul. 🐾

Opposite:
In front of mirrored doors is an antique French wine-tasting table positively groaning under a life's collection of pottery, porcelain, and *objets trouvés*.

Midtown Manhattan Aerie

JANE POOLE is a smart, sophisticated New Yorker, a businesswoman and social arbiter. After her first husband died, she sold the apartment they had lived in in United Nations Plaza in the late 1970s and bought a smaller one. The views may have been breathtaking, but the rooms really were a series of shoe boxes. Jane warned me that my English country house look might not suit the postwar building. She had some good and intriguing antiques and was after a simple, almost modern feeling, but with traditional flair and attention to detail. "All I really asked for specifically," remembers Jane, "was a gray living room—which would suit the building—a pink bedroom, painted floors in the reception areas, and an English feeling of comfort."

We decided to separate the end of the open-plan entry hall and the beginning of the larger living room with architectural elements. These painted-wood Ionic columns and pilasters tied in with overscaled cornices and baseboards. The walls of the hall were papered in a dramatic Chinese red, large-scale, striped and striéd English design. The pièces de résistance were the painted paneled doors, which were faux-grained to resemble mahogany with pearwood and ebony inlays. Displayed on one of the hall walls were Japanese embroideries given by the emperor of Japan to the governor of Missouri at the 1904 St. Louis World's Fair; Jane Poole's family was from St. Louis. Against the other wall were black-lacquered chairs and hall table, the latter holding a large antique Imari jar.

The floors throughout the apartment (except for the bedrooms) were faux-painted in neutral stone and greige colors; the treatment resembled limestone blocks but with the more playful and much cosier feel of wood. The many coats of paint—two layers of a base color, then the specialty painting, and finally four coats of polyurethane—helped disguise the cheaply made parquet floors that

Opposite:
An overscaled chinoiserie table groans under the weight of antique Imari pots; more are sheltered below. Fine Regency elbow chairs display the flamboyant Brighton Pavilion style.

A Chinese opium table of teak stands before a painted Louis XVI settee. Lamp bases are made from tole tea caddies.

came with the apartment. The same painted floor design was used at a larger scale in the living room. The scale changed at the screen of columns, where a stonelike painted threshold imitated what would have occurred in a real stone-floored room. The effect gave a far more modern feel than rugs would have.

The hall led into the coolth of the watercolory living room—a soft, floating, *ton-sur-ton* enclave of varying grays with a few jabs of bright color and pattern. The curtains, of soft gray cotton with a tiny printed stripe, were semitransparent and similar in tone to the walls. Windows in this type of building are always the most difficult to tame. Many have projecting radiators at the bottom, so one cannot take the curtains to the floor—and three-quarter-length curtains always look like a slip that is too long for a dress! So that the curtains could fall to the floor in Jane's apartment, we hung them from behind wide extended cornices. The tonal gray magic of the room fitted its elegantly tailored owner like a glove.

Bandbox-sleek black and gilt Regency elbow chairs were delightfully linear and mingled well with the beautiful Oriental furniture and paintings and with

Opposite:
Architectural elements added to the hall include crown molding, baseboards, columns, and pilasters. The wood floor was painted to resemble stone; the doors, to resemble mahogany inlaid with pearwood and ebony. The vases on gilded Louis XV brackets and the outsize pot on the black-lacquer hall table are seventeenth- and eighteenth-century Imari porcelain.

The octagonal buffet table behind the living room sofa has a shaped, skirted cloth of steel gray satin with inverted pleats at each angle. Gold-lined opaque black lampshades work particularly well in this room; translucent shades would be reflected in the windows at night.

Jane's collection of seventeenth- and eighteenth-century Imari porcelain. Jane said, "I only have pieces with *shishi* on them—Japanese versions of galloping Chinese foo dogs." One of the most interesting pieces of furniture was the carved and painted chinoiserie hall table, clustered à la Daniel Marot (the great Dutch cabinetmaker of the seventeenth and eighteenth centuries) with overscaled Imari pots. Jane Poole had told me, "What I really pine for is a William Kent table— and *neither* of us can afford it!" Certainly a baroque, beswagged, overscaled table would have been perfect, and later, in my downtown wanderings, I found one, tired and abandoned, at a shop called Secondhand Rose. Painted antique bone

white with a *faux-marbre* top and tiny painted Chinese bells, it had great wit and presence—and maybe looked better than the real McKent!

It added up to the perfect soignée single gal pad, beautiful by day and astonishingly glamorous in the evening with Manhattan and the moderne lighting of the Chrysler building glittering outside. The apartment is a perfect place for cocktail parties, which Jane gives with great style, or for a relaxed evening at home. Jane Poole moved into the apartment in 1995. "Keith really did it right," she says. "And I'm as happy there today as when I moved in. He made the shoe box look good!" 🐾

A mélange of plump down-filled cushions dresses the sofa. The leopard-patterned ones were made of Brunschwig's single velvet (most velvets are double velvets like a sandwich, they are sliced through the middle to form the pile), which is woven in France on a hand-operated jacquard loom.

Old-Style Palm Beach

Lee and Allie Hanley's villa in Palm Beach was built in the 1920s by the then fashionable architect Maurice Fatio. He had been described by Billy Baldwin as "an enchanting Swiss fellow," and Cole Porter had written a little ditty about him: "I Want to Live on Maurice Fatio's Patio." He was the great rival of society architect Addison Mizner for the Mediterranean/Hispanic-style houses built for the affluent in Florida and California.

Allie is a vivacious blond and Lee is the tall and handsome scion of a family with connections in oil and building materials; the attractive pair have two pretty daughters. Allie Hanley had visited our office to ask me to look at furniture before her family moved from one lovely Greenwich, Connecticut, house (decorated by Mark Hampton) to another. The Hanleys also have a truly spectacular seagirt 1920s château on a promontory on Fishers Island; it is one of the best houses I have seen in America. Sometimes they use it year-round, but it is mostly a summer base. At around this time—the late 1990s—Lee and Allie found the Fatio house in Florida. Suddenly we were involved with them on three different jobs.

The Florida house, which the family wanted to be its principal residence, was not in good shape; much of the interior architecture had been destroyed. But the Hanleys did manage to procure some original photographs through Fatio's daughter, Alexandra Fatio Taylor, and part of the project involved restoring the main rooms to Fatio's original ideas. The job fell mainly to me and my assistant, Jason Bell, but Lee Hanley proved to be the essential motivator; through his family's business, he was experienced in building and construction. Helped locally by Bill Elias, the on-site construction manager, Lee saw to it that the work was completed in, incredibly, under a year.

Opposite:
The large loggia sunroom, with its soft celadon walls, is furnished with a mix of comfortable old wicker and idiosyncratic painted furniture.

The entrance hall is stippled and glazed in a soft, inviting shade of melon, a key to the rooms that lead off it.

Once the construction and restoration were in progress, we started to plan the interior decoration. The clients, not a bit afraid of color, wanted a vibrant palette and an overall concept that would work for their two daughters. The biggest concern was how to use a vast splendor of fine French and English eighteenth-century antiques that had sat happily in a grand South Ocean Boulevard mansion belonging to Lee's parents. Generationally and geographically, they seemed too fragile for a lively young family, too subtle against the powerful 1920s Hispanic background, and just a bit too tired and old-lady-ish for the new century. But by mixing the furniture in unexpected juxtapositions and re-covering the upholstered pieces with less dowdy fabrics, we moved the interior straight into the twenty-first century.

The entrance hall, with its rough plaster walls and original weathered terra-cotta-tile floor, was almost unadulterated Fatio. My talented Florida "Michelangelo," Brad Brooks, wash-glazed the walls in a lively melon color; he was responsible for all the fine painting in the house. The hall was highlighted by a painted Italian neoclassical console table surmounted by a fine Louis XV painted trumeau mirror.

The vast drawing room had at some time been stripped of its Fatio paneling. We restored the paneled walls and glazed them in three tones of daffodil yellow. This color works well in rooms that do not get a lot of sunlight: during the day, yellow adds a glow to a room, and at night, it positively glistens. The color range was taken from the French print Le Lac, one of Irvine & Fleming's top ten. The yellow damask chinoiserie-style curtains with their tinkling painted Chinese bells and refined Chinese red trimming (created by my master Florida drapery maker Paul Maybaum) are a grateful nod both to Billy Baldwin and to Colonial Williamsburg—where I first saw Chinese shaped valances. On the floor was an exemplary English needlepoint rug. The room enticed visitors all the way to the scintillating French Directoire *bergères* by the fireplace.

The large drawing room with its planked and molded paneled walls. Classic curtains are made of Brunschwig & Fils's Castets silk damask; they are piped in red and have chinoiserie valences with painted bells.

The indoor loggia sunroom, which flowed from and interlocked with the drawing room—a fantastic space for big parties—had an old-fashioned Palm Beach tile floor with sisal rugs, wicker furniture, and palms and lots of other plants. The walls we washed in a celadon green glaze; the beams we stripped down before adding two-tone stenciled designs. We used an English chintz with a dark plum-brown background for almost all the upholstery. Dark chintzes work well in bright, sunny rooms; here, the fabric gave the casual wicker furniture a shot of gravitas. This room was a personal memory of all the great old loggias I saw when I first visited Palm Beach in the late 1950s. I did a house on North Ocean Boulevard for the legendary beauty Aimée de Heeren. I visited it again in 2003—*nothing* had changed in forty-five years, and the owner, now in her nineties, is just as beautiful!

The dining room, which received very little daylight, was designed as a nighttime room. We dark-glazed the old plaster walls in cranberry red. This process produces temporary horror in all clients because the undercoat must be a disgusting, Pepto-Bismol pink. But by the time the top coat is applied, all is usually well.

Neoclassical English chintz curtains play up the drama of the red-glazed walls in the dining room; the Regency-style brown and red carpet holds all the antique furniture together.

Opposite:
In the library, the walls and ceiling are of bleached pecky cypress. Upholstery and curtains are of Trenton Hall, and on the floor is a modern English needlepoint rug.

We built a coffered ceiling, which seemed a very Fatio idea, and filled each square with hand-painted canvas panels I designed—no two alike—with a series of classical and celestial details. They were executed by Dynaflow Studios in Brooklyn, New York. The curtains, in keeping with the theme, were made of an unusual chintz with a neoclassical design of Greek vases and lions. Painted and lacquered Regency armchairs floated around a fine antique Hepplewhite pedestal table, all sitting on a strong brown and red Rocksavage patterned rug from Colefax & Fowler. John Fowler had found an old piece of it at Houghton Hall in Norfolk when he was working there with Lady Cholmondeley. (Houghton is one of my very favorite grand houses in all the world—I have so *many* all-time favorites! The last time Chippy and I visited, I returned to the Stone Hall so many times that the kindly guard said, "You'd really like to buy this house, wouldn't you, Sir? Now you may have your checkbook, but you wouldn't have enough room to write all the naughts required.") The reproduction has always been a great winner at Irvine & Fleming.

The soft and dreamy master bedroom takes its cue from the family's collection of subtle French drawings and watercolors.

The dining room became a dark glowing space, a theatrical setting for candlelight dinners. Dining rooms can be an edge more dramatic than other rooms in a house: guests, there for a limited time, enjoy a heightened atmosphere. This one truly glimmers, making everyone look and feel glamorous. The library, a soothing, composed room, was a mass of Trenton Hall chintz (another love of mine) against pale pickled and glazed pecky cypress walls. With a sedate needlepoint rug and modern wood-frame bookcases wrapped in straw, the room was almost nonexistent but seductive nonetheless.

Upstairs, the master bedroom suite was quite different from the rest of the house. Allie Hanley wanted the room to be gentle and un–Palm Beachy in its soft coloring so that it would not compete with her collection of eighteenth-century French master drawings and watercolors. Walls were stipple-glazed in pale blue—the perfect background for curtains and upholstery in Colefax & Fowler's striped floral linen Lincoln. We paid careful attention to the way the stripes were neatly

On the patio, blue-and-white resist-print cushioned rattan chairs complement the extraordinary Italian tile floor.

centered in the box pleats on the arch-topped valances. A black-ground needlepoint rug and black-lacquered bed were the serious anchors in the romantic room.

A patio in the form of an open-sided breezeway connected the main house to a guest house. Typically Fatio in style, the passage had a tiled roof and a dramatically colored Italian tile floor; furnished with comfortable seating and tables, it was a late-afternoon magnet for the rays of the dipping sun. The patio overlooked a stone-balustraded terrace guarded by giant early-nineteenth-century green-glazed foo dogs. Steps led down to a simple, greenly architectural garden. A cool pool, parallel to the main house, was at the center of a palm-bordered lawn, and a richly tiled fountain beyond provided a focal point.

The Hanley house perpetuated the spirit and allure of Palm Beach without being even a tidge old-fashioned. It is a perfect background for Allie and Lee, who each have one foot confidently in the world of today and the other appreciatively in a glowing past. ❧

Artists in Residence

In the library, a painting by Seward Johnson hangs above a painted Louis XV daybed.

SINCE THE EARLY 1970s, I have worked with Joyce and Seward Johnson Jr. on five projects, all but one in the Princeton area. Joyce is a writer and theater producer, and Seward, the Johnson & Johnson heir, an acclaimed sculptor. I met them through the late William H. Short, an architect in Princeton. Our first collaboration was a house on Newlin Road in Princeton; the next, an apartment in the same historic university town. Irvine & Fleming would also decorate a historic house in Nantucket, an Arts and Crafts–influenced house on Battle Road in Princeton proper, and a new farmhouse nearby.

Beaux-Arts Pied-à-Terre

The apartment in Princeton was in a great old Beaux-Arts mansion, Guernsey Hall. Bill Short was involved in restoring it and dividing it into luxury apartments, and the Johnsons bought one for the times they had too many guests at their Princeton house. A secondary aim was to use the apartment as a dry run for a possible home in Paris—Joyce was a great Francophile. As it happened, Joyce and Seward later lived in Paris for a couple of years but never had a house there.

We put the Guernsey Hall apartment together with a strongly European feeling of luxury, and with much more attention to detail than is customary with many guest houses. The unusual elongated octagon of the living room was further distinguished by a strong architectural framework and elements including massive bookcases on the long sides of the room. These bookcases were trim-glazed in a dark cream to blend with the walls, covered in cream and white French wallpaper with a tiny pattern. The curtains were serenely grand, made of heavy silk woven in champagne, oyster, and cream stripes. An unusual carved-wood and gilt gesso

Opposite:
The floral hand-blocked English chintz on the living room sofa is a Cowtan & Tout fabric; when we did the apartment, it was still a small, almost unknown firm.

French painted and decorated tole and brass beds set the tone in a guestroom. At the foot of each was an iron bench topped with a folded American quilt.

French mantelpiece anchored the fireplace wall; above was a lovely English Regency landscape looking glass. These mirrors, with a painted landscape for the top panel and a larger plain mirror beneath, are nearly always used to complement a mantelpiece. The landscape in this case was a reverse-painted Chinese panel.

The overstuffed furniture, upholstered in a warm floral hand-blocked English chintz, sat on an exemplary English nineteenth-century needlepoint rug. An eighteenth-century carved-wood and parcel-gilt Austrian chandelier hung from the ceiling. Many of the painted and fruitwood elbow chairs were eighteenth-century French. The ensemble was quiet but sophisticated.

One of the bedrooms was a pure late-nineteenth-century French set piece. Two nineteenth-century French painted metal twin beds instantly established the mood. The striped floral wallpaper would have enchanted Colette's *salon,* and along with the French drawings on the walls and the airy white French cotton-lace curtains—heightened with an 1880s crystal fringe—created a room Misia Sert could have slept in.

The tiny library / study had a comfortable background of dark beige glazed bookcases and natural Madagascar straw-cloth wall covering. Hanging above a recessed daybed covered in raspberry silk-mohair velvet was an early nude painting by Seward himself. On the floor was a gray rabbit rug—we were not so knowledgeable about animal rights in those days. The little bathroom was mirrored everywhere, a shimmering maze of multiple reflections reminiscent of the hall of mirrors scene in *The Lady from Shanghai* with Rita Hayworth and Orson Welles. The Johnsons had to use bright scarlet towels to find their way around!

154

Outside was a projecting terrace of some size; because the apartment was three floors up, it became a hanging garden. The terrace overlooked splendid specimen trees on the surrounding estate. We custom-built wood benches based on the famous Lutyens model—this was before the Lutyens version became commercially available. The benches were set into the stone walls that surrounded the terrace. Often a table and chairs were drawn up to one of the benches for an alfresco meal. Seat cushions were burnt orange canvas—just like Elsie de Wolfe's in her Villa Trianon garden in Versailles (where a private gate led to the park of the château). The floor of the terrace was tiled in a geometric Roman-style pattern—good old American Olean tiles. They looked amazingly neoclassical and spirited—and stood up so well to the elements.

Our replica of the Lutyens garden bench offers seating on the terrace, as do English nineteenth-century white-painted wire garden chairs.

On the Beach

As the colorful 1960s turned into the somewhat blah 1970s (the same time we were working on the Guernsey Hall apartment, in fact), the Johnsons found a beautiful, late-nineteenth-century shingle-style two-story house on a great beachfront property on Nantucket. With help from Bill Short (and after much to-ing and fro-ing with the local planning board and preservation office), the Johnsons moved the house closer to the beach. It was jacked up one whole floor on a new foundation to create a three-story structure. The new ground-floor "basement" was encased in a series of heavy shuttered panels that made it seem as if the shingle house was magically lifted off the ground, and a fine old-style veranda around the main house—now the second floor—enhanced the views of the ocean.

The interior of the old house was mostly gutted and redone according to Joyce and Seward's ideas, notably with a lot of natural-wood-paneled walls. Seward's orders to me: "Keith, I want the house to feel as if you could sweep it out with a broom, and everything in it should look as if it had arrived in Nantucket on a clipper ship."

Leading to a large living room and a small sitting room was a truly tiny entrance hall—maybe the most favorite space I have ever *ever* created. Above a dark glazed dado, the walls were covered in antique canvas panels painted with a romantic scene: an ancient port, overhung by a cragged castle and surrounded by a sea scattered with approaching sailing ships. The literary vision was a far cry from the reality of Nantucket's now restored harbor.

The double-height living room had soothing wood walls and soft, off-white linen curtains on simple iron rods. The comfortable furniture was covered in heavy stone-colored Irish linen with a thick, soothing texture. Fine early American furniture spiced with unexpected and eclectic pieces from Egypt, Java, Bali, China, and Japan gave the living room an easy, casual, and most of all, timeless feeling. Most of the rugs throughout the house were cotton dhurries from India or Tibet and the most spectacular was the unusual, large Indian-made Art Deco rug with a strong yellow background in the living room. Close to the ceiling was an inexpensive cubic American kite—I still wonder how on earth Gary Zarr, then my assistant, and I ever got it up there. A staircase ascended from the living room to a flying bridge, which led to two children's rooms on one side and two guest rooms on the other. Heavy natural wood shutters on the upper windows could be raised or lowered by a pulley and rope system—a traditional nautical device—from the flying bridge.

The little sitting room was in part a memory of what the house might have felt like in its early days. The background was painted off-white Edwardian-looking Philadelphia siding; a crown molding just above eye level forms a display shelf. Off-white painted bookcases reach to the same height, a particularly Edwardian aspect. The curtains and the Roman shade over the window seat were in a cool sky blue and white cotton print; though now slightly dated, it still looks pretty good! The seat pads of the old bleached wicker chairs and the

View of the Johnsons' gray shingled house from the tennis pavilion. The new ground floor with its heavy green-painted shutters raised the house by one story. White painted steps lead to the main living floor.

Opposite:
A practical rope and pulley system, borrowed from old-time sailing ships, operates the shutters in the living room.

In the sitting room, sky-blue linen upholstery is offset by the elusive but suave coloring of the dhurrie.

upholstered furniture were covered in pale blue linen with white piping. The tufted sofa was covered in a batik with an intense orange ground I had found in Bali. On the floor was an Indian dhurrie in an unusual combination of muted stone-washed lavender, blue, and peach. A model of a Chinese junk sails across the top of one bookcase.

The master bedroom, also on the former ground floor, was serene and simple: pale wood walls and bleached muslin curtains look out to a typical northeast coastal fog. The porch furniture is just visible as a company of ghostly shapes in the mist. The large bedroom rug was one of my well-loved Irish linen ones; its

Simple muslin curtains, an Irish linen rug, a tufted sofa, and an American quilt are the essential ingredients of the master bedroom.

subtle blue and white looked pleasingly used even when brand new. The large "fainting" sofa was covered in an orangey Indienne chintz, and the bed cover was a vintage American yo-yo quilt.

The wide porches were scattered with old weathered wood and wicker furniture. Where it overlooked the garden, the porch was screened to make a semi-outdoor breakfast room that connected with the kitchen. The shingles on the three walls surrounding this area were preweathered to the perfect Nantucket gray. Sitting on a thickly woven natural rush rug were a built-in china cabinet, an American pine trestle table, and painted chairs with old rustic wood and Shaker

woven seats. An American hooked rug—a dog with the legend "man's best friend"—hung on the wall.

On the new ground floor were two distinct rooms, one a cheery, child-friendly family room, the other a billiard room. The former, bright and inviting, had an early-1970s flavor with natural modern wicker furniture and brightly colored, geometrically patterned American cotton fabrics. It even had one of those 1960s hanging plastic swing chairs! Bottle green shutters on the outside walls could be opened with the push of a button.

The billiard room was a 1970s interpretation of a nineteenth-century men's club. It sported an early-twentieth-century pool table. An observation and lounging area with overscaled leather banquette sofas scattered with batik throw pillows was raised on a carpeted dais.

When the house was ready for its first summer, Joyce Johnson tracked me down in Bel Air, California, where I was working on a new job. She said, "It is everything we all talked about, but way beyond our dreams—a house for the rest of our lives!" This has proved very true. It was modern when it was put together, but it has become timeless. When I dropped by for a drink more than a quarter of a century later, I found the house almost completely unchanged. As we passed through the sitting room, I exclaimed, "Oh, you moved that chair!"

Dream Farmhouse

A few years after the Nantucket house, I worked on a house in Princeton for the Johnsons, again with Bill Short. Sadly, he was to die shortly thereafter. Then, late in the summer of 2002, I was having a nostalgic dinner with Seward and Joyce when they mentioned that they were having problems with a new farmhouse they were building on a large estate nearby. Apparently it was all stop and start, with endless changes and alterations. They were working with architect David Schultz of Philadelphia. His wife, Susan Davidson, had designed the Johnsons' restaurant near Trenton, Rat's, which was named after Water Rat's burrow in the children's classic *The Wind in the Willows*. Susan had also helped with two guest cabins on the farm and a cottage interior.

The billiard room has electronic shutters to control natural light.

Opposite:
Screens and preweathered gray shingles enclose a breakfast room.

By this time, though, Joyce had almost completely lost interest in the new farmhouse. I think maybe Seward thought that since I had worked with them for almost a quarter of a century, I might be able to jump-start the farmhouse—and off we went. The Johnsons, my English assistant, Felicity Wilde, and I immediately injected new life into the project. Seward later told Chippy, "Altogether there were forty-seven *major* changes that required a total reorganization of the additions. We really missed time not working with Keith."

The house, though newly built, was designed to look like a country farmhouse that had changed gradually over the last couple of hundred years. The house sat among some trees in a lovely high fold of land surrounded by sheep meadows with a great stand of woods at the back of the fold. The land in front of the house rolled down to a distant pond, then to a far vista. "I am wild and flamboyant," said Seward. "Joyce is muted. She was always shrinking the house, reducing the silhouette. We wanted graciousness without splendor—a country home, not a grand estate."

A dark-green-lacquered heavy paneled door led from the wide porch that ran the length of the front of the house into a two-story-high great room. "We learned from the Nantucket house how civilized it was to practically live on the porch," Seward said. "We also knew that with a porch, the living room would be dark unless it was two stories high." The two levels of windows flooded the living room with light. Throughout the soaring space, these shafts of light caught different facets of the seemingly old beam structure with its convincingly rough, hand-textured plastered walls. Carefully selected old weathered timber, with would-be peg holes and adze cuts, came from Vintage Beams and Timbers in North Carolina.

The overscaled rough fireplace was proportioned to suit Seward, who loves blazing fires, and to complement massive early-nineteenth-century Continental andirons and tools. The fireplace was a perfect spot for an enormous French eighteenth-century decorated fireback we had found for the Johnsons' last Princeton house. These cast-iron beauties, used to throw the heat of the fire forward, were found in great houses in the past and were often decorated with family crests and emblems. They are almost unused today, although the

Opposite:
The antiqued and distressed chimney breast in the living room has bookcases on either side made of old timber. A wing chair is covered in a hand-embroidered Chelsea Editions fabric made in India. The pattern was based on an English crewel design. In front of the chair is an Indonesian bench (it reminds me of an execution block!) used as a footrest.

On an early-nineteenth-century French chaise are a 1920s Navajo blanket throw and a cockerel pillow, painted by Chippy, based on one of Seward Johnson's oils.

Johnsons have one in every fireplace in the house. Perched on the rough beam mantel was an antique French iron cockerel—one of Seward's favorite motifs, and one that appeared in almost every Johnson house.

The brick chimney breast was a story in itself. We had decided that this part of the room should look as if most of the paint and some of the plaster had fallen off over the course of its life and times, thus revealing the old brick. So one morning, I, at seventy-five, joined the young master plasterer on a frightfully wobbly scaffold to work out how much plaster might have fallen. I like to believe I gradually gained "cred" with the crew: they silently stopped working to watch me, this old guy in natty tweed jacket and bow tie, on top of the two-story scaffold. Then it was up the scaffold again with my master painter, Lester Drozd, to finish the textured plaster. In the midst of antiquing and glazing, we decided to try the look of an old roof leak. The glaze was dragged, wiped vertically, and yellowed a bit—very effective, just like a movie set. (Not such a far-fetched idea. In the early 1960s, I was approached by Sam Spiegel to do the sets for a big-time Hollywood movie, *55 Days at Peking*. The carrot was the fact that his next caper was to be *Marie Antoinette*—though it was never made. After a couple of meetings, however, we realized that we were way out of our depth—though the possibility of meeting Ava Gardner was hard to pass up.) The end of this long faux-painting procedure in the Johnson farmhouse came when the builder, who knew nothing about our paint job, was completely taken in. He told Seward, "I'm afraid there has been a leak down the new chimney breast. I'll have to repair it." Seward and all of us had a good laugh at that!

But I digress. The living room, a *ton-sur-ton* tour de force, was a collection of memories from a familiar past, eclectic but with an air of history. Like the Johnsons' beach house in Nantucket, it was a world-encompassing conglomeration of Joyce and Seward's shared interests. A painted Swedish elbow chair, a rather severe but lovely old French fruitwood chaise longue, a beautifully worn North Chinese altar table, a straw Indonesian trunk with a lacquered-wood frame, two old Orkney chairs near the fireplace (my Scottish injection), all mixed with good American antiques: call it "Around the World in Eighty Ways." The mélange was grounded with Guatemalan rugs in subdued colors with different weaves and designs. The upper space of the living room was pierced by two gargantuan, two-tiered, carved- and painted-wood, rustic rococo chandeliers. They could be lowered by an electronic winch for cleaning and to change bulbs—*hélas, pas de chandelles!*

Also on the ground floor was a tiny library with paneling and bookcases of elm. A large sofa was covered in a bold English print on linen from Clarence House, and two small swivel chairs—Keith chairs, the only piece of furniture named after me—were upholstered in beige linen. There was also a leather lounge chair and ottoman and an unusual rug from Guatemala made of leather woven with fine strips of wood. I had never seen one like it before or since. The rough plaster ceiling was glazed in a dirty aquamarine, a tone pulled from the English printed linen. From the old beams hung an eighteenth-century linnet birdcage (the song of the linnets was once highly desirable background music) wired as a lantern. This is a trick I have repeated many times—when the cage is lighted, it casts an alluring spider's web shadow on the ceiling.

A "tablescape" on a rustic Dutch seventeenth-century inlaid table includes a real bird's nest with a faux egg. Chippy and I gave it to Joyce and Seward as a housewarming present. It is guarded by an eighteenth-century Chelsea wood pigeon.

The small elm-paneled den with recessed bookcases and an antique birdcage wired as a chandelier.

A robust staircase ascended from the living room to a gallery/library/landing with bookcases fashioned from vintage oak timbers—Henry Higgins in a rustic setting. Readers could hurl acerbic comments at a conversation below while searching for a particular book. The landing led to the Johnsons' private wing. The master bedroom, one of the most peaceful rooms I have ever put together, was like a watercolor of an old French country room. "It's simple and subtle at the same time," said Seward. "There's always something for the eye to linger on. Keith will have a pillow made in a print, then redye it to make it even better." A pale, close-to-nonexistent blue, beige, and white printed cotton was combined with washed-out sprigged wallpaper from Colefax; both played against soft

In the master bedroom is a French provincial walnut mantel. The blue and white sprigged Colefax & Fowler wallpaper is outlined by antique distressed beams.

bleached oak beams. With its six windows, the room had a painterly quality of light at every moment of the day. Where am I, a visitor might wonder. Mougins? Aix-en-Provence? Anet? It was some lovely French house from the past. The art was personal and included a portrait by Seward of the Johnsons' son, Johnnie, as an infant.

The master bedroom connected with a tiny and pensive bathroom. The stepped tub was positioned high so that bathers could simultaneously soak and brood on the sheep dotting the greensward outside. The bluish-gray *imprimé* wallpaper was French; the wood floor, painted in sun-faded faux marble. The adjoining private sitting room was relaxed and comfortable. It revolved around

a naive hand-blocked English thin linen tree-of-life print—brilliantly cheap looking but in reality *so* expensive. It was from Robert Kime, the decorator for Prince Charles.

Seward and Joyce had specifically asked for two facing one-armed uphol-stered chaises before the fireplace "so we can talk and hold hands"—not a request we get too often. A marvelous American hooked rug depicting a fox became the "genius of the place"; the animal seemed to point to the bay window with its green-leather buttoned seat pad and throw pillows. Over an American maple drop-leaf desk behind the chaises was the Regency reverse-painted landscape mirror that we first bought for Guernsey Hall.

I did not design the farmhouse kitchen—Chippy says I should not be let near a kitchen, even though she admits I make them *look* marvelous, and in this case, I did help with the decoration. Both the kitchen and its adjoining breakfast room were joyously sunny, prompting many hearty smiles. Though the kitchen was full of state-of-the-art technology, the effect was of Juan-les-Pins or Cap-Ferrat—never the New Jersey countryside! The area glowed from the egg-yolk yellow of the hand-made, built-to-order La Cornue range—the Rolls-Royce of gas stoves. Above the center island was a copper and steel *batterie de cuisine*. The wood floor was stenciled in a faded parquetry design echoing the colors in the tiled back-splash. At the far end, in a bay window overlooking the pool barn and sheep meadow, was an old American farmhouse pine table surrounded by ladder-back chairs and an antique painted Swedish settee. Above the table was a time-worn, rusted iron chandelier with white porcelain tulip candle holders, similar to one Chippy and I had in our cottage living room at St. Johns Farm. They were not antiques; in fact, they were made in the Bronx. The rough stone mantel was carved in Italy, and above it was a lovely Jean Cocteau drawing most definitely coveted by Felicity and myself!

A guest room in the farmhouse was fresh and simple. Its old bleached-oak beams enhanced the off-white strié wallpaper; the theme fabric was Colefax's off-white and green English chintz called Bowood—miles of it. It is one of John Fowler's top ten (and also the print used in my mother's bedroom in Richmond, England). There was a lot of easygoing, good antique American furniture. The

Opposite:
In the private sitting room are two custom-made chaises with one arm each covered in a Robert Kime linen print. The landscape mirror over the desk is an old friend from a previous Johnson house.

On the stair landing are a ticking-covered armchair, a Swedish side chair, and a sculpture from Seward Johnson's atelier.

only slightly odd, but very pretty, intruders were two fine antique Hepplewhite painted and decorated elbow chairs. Any guest would feel instantly at home in the green peace of this room.

Now fasten your seat belts! Below the house was an amazing three-level theater/playroom/lounge area entered via a hidden staircase from the living room. The lowest zone was an arena for performances and for the large movie screen hidden behind natural linen curtains. The vast rug was of thick wool, natural in color and custom-woven in Tibet. The next level, full of comfortable sofas and overlooking the theater area, was perfect for movies or perhaps the endless games of charades so loved by the Johnsons. The highest level was a large space divided into a games area, a seating group in front of the fire, and an ample bar.

The walls near the fireplace were roughly plastered and then hand-waxed with beeswax to give an effect of age—a successful technique I have often used. These walls blended well with the weathered beams. Seward and Joyce's concept for the playroom plus was to have optimum comfort with seemingly rough edges—as Seward put it, "a hint of Zen and a dash of Navajo." Joyce says, "I did, and *do,* have ideas. The great thing about Keith was that he listened to them. He was able to make use of the strengths I had in ideas—and could fill in the gaps without letting me feel it! So they became reality. He was tuned into our—and my—taste." In the case of the fire surround, we decided that it should have the structural feeling of a Zen gate. Seward took an old envelope and, in about seven strokes, sketched a design; some months later, the exact image, in three dimensions, sat in place.

Felicity Wilde designed a contemplative yet contemporary Zenlike bar with stone-tiled counters. Above it were shelves for bottles; supports were hidden so that the shelves appeared to float against a backlit wall of natural Japanese straw tatami. Refrigerator, dishwasher, ice maker, and storage were under the bar, concealed by horizontal strips of antiqued wood; cutout grips ensured that no surface hardware was visible. Water flowed from a high bronze spigot into a rough, basinlike sink carved from solid marble. A heavy serving block could be moved around on its immense casters.

Most walls of the room were insulated and lined, then covered in a natural-colored, knobbly Irish Donegal tweed called Black Sheep. It was a mixture of all the tones of the wild sheep on the westernmost coasts of Ireland and Scotland. When I came across the tweed in America, it was a blast from the past, a fabric more or less out of fashion for fifty years. I had owned a super (quite noticeable, says Chippy the fashionista) greatcoat made of it in the early 1950s! Most of the overstuffed furniture was also covered in Black Sheep. Strange and rather crude but effective wall sconces were forged out of heavy iron in what is best described as *Planet of the Apes* style. Felicity had discovered a pair of the sconces, made in the mid-twentieth century, and we had the rest copied. An Oriental black-lacquered card table was surrounded by shiny lipstick-red-leather high-back chairs; additional spots of red—cushions, quilts, and objects—were scattered throughout the space.

In the kitchen, a rectangular pine table is used for breakfast and informal meals. The stone mantel was carved in Italy. The wood floor was faux-painted to resemble parquet in tones that match the tiles in the rest of the kitchen.

The bar in the three-level lounge features horizontal wood elements and concealed door and drawer handles. Both the bar and the movable serving trolley have stone counters. The lighting that shines through natural Japanese straw cloth can be lowered or heightened for dramatic effect.

The floor was enlivened by rugs in three different Navajo patterns. Even the powder room had a wall screen, so that the movie being shown on the big screen could be viewed. The three-level space constituted an enticing destination for family gatherings, large theatrical happenings, or quiet contemplative interludes.

The pool barn, designed by David Schultz and carried through with Jay Rockafella and Susan Davidson, had little to do with Irvine & Fleming, but it was one of the most successful buildings on the estate. The first time I saw its stone walls and rusty red tin roof, I thought it was an old building left on the site—certainly not one that was newly constructed. Inside was a long pool that glistened from its black tile lining along with the attendant hot tubs, saunas, and exercise rooms. One wall of the pool house was all glass and overlooked the sheep meadow. The sheep must enjoy watching the swimmers inside! The walls and

Opposite:
We translated Seward's design for a Zen gate fireplace into reality with old timber and accents of rusty iron.

An Amish quilt in rainbow colors and Navajo pots accent the muted tone of the Black Sheep tweed fabric.

Opposite:
The rough stone and vintage wood pool house has a black-tile-lined pool and a lounging area with painted wicker and natural rattan pieces.

high ceilings, made of found old timber, pick up and throw around the almost cathedral-like shafts of light—so alluring.

Seward has commented, "Whenever our friends come here, or young people, such as my son's cohorts from his Eyebeam digital museum—they are hard-edged, abstract, and sophisticated, dedicated to bringing science and art together—well, they love it and are absorbed by the carefully considered details." I must say that it warms the cockles of my decorator's heart to have worked so often and so long for such rewarding, intellectual, and deep-thinking clients as Joyce and Seward Johnson. Seward's one-man show at the Corcoran Gallery in Washington in 2003 was a major success, and now he has taken to painting—of interiors in particular. Joyce has become involved with theater production. The repartee at our meetings was pure gold. Seward always says, "We are all three artists"; to which I add, "Yes, and now real old friends." 🐱

Mayfair by the Sea

The enfilade of three halls. The first entry hall is centered on a Florentine hand-painted and gilt chandelier. The second is an octagonal entry space; and the third is a dark-glazed area furnished with an upholstered and fretted chinoiserie lacquered daybed.

Opposite:
An inlaid Italian marble top sits on a modern altar table in the first hall. On the marble floor is an antique Chinese rug, rare because of its unusual colors.

I N THE 1990s, my clients Leslie and Margie Rose bought a stuccoed villa on the old Phipps estate in Palm Beach; in its heyday, the property had stretched from the ocean to the bay, but it was gradually broken up after World War II. The villa's white-painted facade had a cool, clean appearance with a lofty pedimented portico. In South Florida real estate parlance, it is called "Regency"—though it is light years away from the early-nineteenth-century Regency seaside villas of Brighton or Sidmouth in England.

The calm facade only hinted at the grandeur inside. The Roses, who hail from Detroit, came to me through a client there for whom I had created a luxe Anglo-Russian gem of a duplex—a tiny *trianon* à la Pavlovsk. Leslie and Margie were familiar with my Anglo-American style but were looking for more of a flight of fantasy for their house in Palm Beach, something perhaps whimsical in the vein of Oliver Messel's classically inspired beach houses in Barbados and Mustique but in a practical, bandbox-fresh American way. Joining forces with me on the project was my then assistant, Edwin Jackson.

Once we had worked with the clients to establish the overall mood for each room, Edwin and I played with a progression of contrasting and connecting colors leading from room to room, a signature of Irvine & Fleming's work. The arched enfilades that marched through the center of the house provided the perfect backdrop. "The house had been on the market for some time," said Margie Rose, "because nobody had the insight or imagination to know what to do with these three successive halls. Keith with his great color sense solved it."

Once the project was moving ahead, Edwin and I took off for London and spent a week searching for antiques and art. Edwin remembers: "The working relationship between Keith and myself spanned more than seven years. I have

177

Flattering coral walls and a hand-painted, un-draped four poster bed combined with the bird of paradise chintz in the master bedroom.

often told him his greatest attribute is his unwavering enthusiasm and passion for his work. His greatest strengths as an interior decorator are his sense of color and his breaking of 'the rules' to create a relaxed and undecorated atmosphere. Keith taught without teaching, sharing his life experiences, his love of history, books, and old movies."

The Roses joined us in London, and in a two-day spree, we bought every antique needed to finish the house. These ran the gamut from pieces of staggering

Opposite:
Chinese red-lacquered settee set in mirrored bookcase alcove.

top quality to less grand but unusual and amusing items. One of the peaks was a carved-wood and parcel-gilt chinoiserie Thomas Chippendale overmantel. Its decorative panels had been reverse-painted in China in the 1780s, when the Chippendale workshop had a lucrative importing business based there, and brought to London by ship. Our greatest coup was finding a museum-quality inlaid marble mantel that fit the overmantel exactly. Robert Adam had it carved and inlaid by Pietro Bossi, the outstanding eighteenth-century Italian carver who operated out of Dublin, for a grand Irish house. Bossi was, at the time, said to be the most famous marble carver in the world. The Roses almost did not get the mantel. Britain was loath to lose yet another piece of its heritage to the "revolting colonies," but after months of delay and frustration, the export license was granted and Mr. Adam's mantel was on its way to a new home in Florida.

Unbeknownst to all of us at the time, the decoration on the mantel, quite an unusual design for Robert Adam, would become the leitmotif of a theme that eventually ran through the whole house. Inspired by the mantel's inlaid birds—no two alike—we decided to paint the expansive tray ceiling in the vast, ballroom-size drawing room (I called it the saloon, after the Italian *salone,* a room for social interaction—for what we might today call "working the room") as a trompe l'oeil bamboo pergola. The pergola was populated with a flock of multicolored birds; a few passed by the ravishing eighteenth-century Waterford crystal chandelier on their migration from one end of the room to the other. A bar was hidden inside a Chinese lacquer armoire made from an eight-panel eighteenth-century Coromandel screen. Impeccably constructed, the armoire opened to reveal a sleek arrangement of black lacquer

Two white-on-white textured wool rugs from Spain partially cover the white marble floor of the large saloon, or drawing room, designed for entertaining. The circular fringed ottoman, which can be split into segments, is covered with a striped needlepoint fabric from Clarence House.

Opposite:
The tour de force Robert Adam mantel is topped by an equally tour de force Chippendale landscape mirror.

The bar in the saloon was made from antique Coromandel screen panels found in London.

Opposite:
On the dining table is an extravagant Louis XV *surtout de table*, or *plafond*. It holds candles and, on this occasion, mixed roses.

and mirrored glass. Two more eighteenth-century Chinese paneled screens, teeming with tree peonies and songbirds, harmoniously colored in a golden apricot and in perfect condition, flanked the chimney breast.

Edwin and I calmed these top-drawer antiques with good, straightforward English pieces and lots of comfy chintz-covered overstuffed furniture. The walls and trim were faux-painted to imitate blocks of creamy honey-toned limestone complete with artistically dilapidated cracks and breaks. Both clients and designers wanted to intimate that the room had been re-formed from a sun-drenched ruin. The final dressing to the lively and eclectic drawing room was the set of curtains, swagged, jaboted, and draped, with magnificent trimming and tassels. Unlike their grand Paris or London forebears, however, these were made out of unlined creamy silk-linen striped gauze, elegant and floaty in any passing breeze. Emma, Lady Hamilton, and Lord Nelson had, I hope, curtains like this in their palazzo in Palermo. The curtains were in part inspired by drawings by the talented and much-beloved English artist and set designer Rex Whistler for Lady Catherine de Bourgh's saloon for the London stage production of *Pride and Prejudice* in the 1930s.

As always, another almost semi-unconscious influence was that of my mentor, John Fowler, who never visited Palm Beach, let alone America. One much-repeated anecdote had Mrs. Paul Mellon trying to lure Fowler to both Virginia and Manhattan. She was perhaps not quite on her knees but close, offering private jets and so forth. His terse reply? "Bunny, I don't have *time* left to waste on that silly country!"

The wallpaper and upholstery in the private sitting area of the master bedroom extended the bird and flower theme that runs throughout the house.

Opposite:
In the breakfast room, the Swedish-style painted table and chairs sit on a striped wool rug. Above a French provincial cabinet is an arrangement of ceramic plates.

Walls in the sumptuous dining room were covered in a hand-blocked French wallpaper simulating drapery; the border of ceiling swags was designed in an artlessly nonrealistic manner. The curtains were toile de Jouy in a neoclassical design. On one wall was an 1830 Dufour painted panel depicting the story of Pelléas and Mëlisande; in front of it was a William IV sideboard that had been made for the great house Saltram in Devon. Less formal meals were taken in the trellis-papered breakfast room. Its curtained, arched French doors led out to a tropical garden.

The master bedroom, with walls and upholstery covered in a bird-of-paradise pattern, reiterated the avian motif. The walls were outlined in a double bamboo border in an unexpected shade of blue-green. Two gilded and painted nineteenth-century French armoires provided the necessary luxury, while heavy white matelassé curtains, trellis-patterned carpeting, and overstuffed furniture provided the necessary comfort. "Keith insisted on doing the house without me being there," says Margie Rose. "Then he called and told me I could come home. When I saw it, I just couldn't believe I was living there. It couldn't have been prettier."

In a witty article about the Roses' house written for *House Beautiful* in September 2000, Martin Filler set down the "genealogy of decoration." As he wrote, "when and where who works for whom" is key to understanding the transmission of taste from the *haut décor* of Europe across the Atlantic to the most rarified precincts of America—in this case, Palm Beach. (To give credit where it is due, I must note that I borrowed Filler's amusing and apt title for this chapter.)

Park Avenue Principessa

S IBILLA TOMACELLI CLARK is a Neapolitan-born *principessa*, skilled hostess, international charmer—and my favorite and most enduring client. She's the tops! I love her Italian warmth, resourcefulness, and style. Over the years, I have worked with her on five different projects: two New York apartments, a London town house, an eighteenth-century house in the old town on Nassau, Bahamas, and a new house in Lyford Cay. She is the greatest recommender, and in this business, recommendation is key. She understands how the game is played.

Refreshingly, Sibilla is not obsessed with interior decoration. She is far more interested in the comfort and interplay of her guests, and in using her various "backgrounds" as settings for entertaining. When she bought her Park Avenue apartment in the 1980s, she and I agreed that it was a dingy, depressing mess. The worst feature was a long, grim, very wide entrance hall with a black and white linoleum floor. Six undistinguished doors leading to various rooms imparted a drab institutional effect. Sibilla and I fast decided to develop the hall as an architectural library since there was no real library space in the apartment. I was inspired by memories of a grand library hall created by Georges Geffroy for Stavros Niarchos in Paris in the early 1950s (though the rest of the house was decorated by Emilio Terry). Sibilla's hall became a neoclassical fantasy of grained woods, gilding, porphyry columns, and ivory inlays—all faux. Niarchos's, of course, was all real!

Entrances to the various rooms alternated with little niches for bookcases, cupboards, writing desk and chair, telephone area, bar, media paraphernalia, and tiny conversational area with settee. Upon entering the apartment for the first big cocktail party, Kenneth Jay Lane, the Manhattan socialite and jewelry designer, exclaimed, "I must have the wrong palazzo!"

Opposite:
A specially built arch in the library hall accommodates two carved and gilded dragons on their own plinths.

187

The elements of the library hall combined to form a grand and amusing enfilade that led to the very European drawing room. The arch at the far end of the hall was emphasized by two fantasy wood and gilded-tole Regency dragons in Brighton Pavilion style, an extravagant wedding present found at Mallett's in London. The drawing room was a traditional and eclectic mix of mostly English and Italian antiques, many scrounged from Sibilla's grand London town house. The walls were papered in an *imprimé* Italian paper with a tiny pattern; contrasting wallpaper borders and painted striping defined the walls, dramatizing the cornice and adding a feeling of height to the room. The ceiling was stipple-glazed in pale lavender, one of the many colors in the hand-blocked floral English glazed chintz covering the overstuffed sofa and armchairs.

Opposite:
The great drawing room stretches from one side of the building to the other. It has windows at each end, which gives it a great quality of light, a rarity in most Manhattan apartments.

A marble bust dominates the classical "mantelscape"; a convex Regency mirror reflects the room.

A wallpaper border gives the butler's pantry a decorative paneled effect. The drawing room beyond is dominated by a huge nineteenth-century pastel portrait of King Charles II. I found the portrait in a dilapidated, water-damaged state, and Chippy restored it.

We hung an early-eighteenth-century Italian portrait on a panel of mirrored glass exactly the width of the sofa—an old trick that throws light around a room and creates the subliminal effect of an archway to a room beyond. Hanging pictures and sconces on the silvered glass blocks guests from preening; and after dark, the sconces double the glitter. The heavy double-lined "London" curtains (my term for this sort of sumptuous arrangement) of cream corded cotton with deep red fringe were Regency in style, and pure John Fowler; after all, Fowler had decorated the great Moyns Park house in Essex, England, for Sibilla's mother-in-law, Jo Hartford Bryce. The room was anchored by two dark-ground antique rugs—one a Bessarabian based on a Victorian floral design and the other a French needlepoint that was pure "Spectre de la Rose"—on a good oak floor.

Opposite:
This "tablescape" in the drawing room includes an English Staffordshire shepherd and one of Sibilla's many fans. The Italian gouache depicts a classical mythical subject.

191

Connected to the drawing room is an intimate dining area that had once been office space. The eighteenth-century dog painting was bought at a Sotheby's auction. A tufted chair in the foreground is covered in Dame du Lac toile, which is based on *The Lady of the Lake* by Sir Walter Scott.

The previous owner of the apartment had a secretary's office tucked behind one wall of the drawing room. We replaced the wall with an arched opening to create a dining alcove that could be served from the butler's pantry. Walls were upholstered in champagne silk; champagne-striped gauze balloon shades draped the windows; the lambrequin was trimmed with real Regency bullion fringe. A good, plain English table was pushed up to an extravagantly upholstered, painted Louis XVI–style canapé—really just a piece of "junque" from a thrift shop in Southampton, New York—and some "just okay" black-lacquer Regency chairs Sibilla had picked up at Worlds End, at the far end of the Kings Road in London, where there are several small antique and bric-a-brac shops. Sharing a meal in the dining alcove, tiny yet theatrical and romantic, was almost like having supper in an opera box.

Every inch of the master bedroom—even the ceiling—was papered in an English design with a small blue and white pattern; a matching wallpaper border outlined and defined the room. The border criss-crossed the ceiling, so that the bedroom felt like the interior of a pretty papered box. This is another great old trick—but more difficult in these days of fewer wallpaper borders. The effect was sweet and feminine. In fact, all bedrooms should be feminine, I believe. Men especially love this feeling. It is, after all, an extension of what they find most alluring in their wives!

The tufted sleigh bed and the curtains were in another classic English chintz, and painted wood bells touched the valences with chinoiserie detailing. The dressing table was the most feminine thing in this feminine room, a froth of three varieties of *broderie anglaise* with pointed rose-colored scallops. I had seen photographs of one that Mariga Guinness had made with her own hands for the master bedroom at Leixlip Castle in Ireland in the early 1950s. In the photo, it was held together rather crudely with white pushpins. Sibilla, who had known Mrs. Guinness well, loved the idea, and I persuaded Chippy to re-create it—but without the pushpins. It absolutely must be as full as the skirt of the organdy dress Dior made for Princess Margaret's twenty-first birthday, I told Chippy. "Thank good-ness for Velcro," she said, but Chippy had such a job stuffing the table skirt into a taxi that it almost stayed in our apart-ment. Sibilla's room typifies my favorite bedroom combina-tion: two different patterned English chintzes, an undemand-ing little *fleurette* wallpaper with its border, and an assortment of soft but not obvious cushions—one in Victorian needle-point, another in a tiny blue taffeta stripe, a third in an allover seaweed chintz.

One of my very favorite details is this corner of Sibilla's bedroom with its Regency recamier and its variety of soft cushions.

Sibilla's Park Avenue apartment was my homage to Sir John Soane, Charles de Beistegui, and Luchino Visconti—the last being one of the great dilettante decorators of the twen-tieth century. And Sibilla was, and is, fabulous to work with—beautiful, quick, considerate, and very "Italian thrifty," a quality that as a Scotsman I much admire. "One of Keith's best qualities, though perhaps I shouldn't mention it," Sibilla says, "is that he doesn't push expensive things. Of course, that quality might put off the nouveau riche."

Sibilla put her clever hands to many small details in the apartment—in her Nassau house, she made all the curtains herself. "Keith never forced any decora-tion on me that I didn't want—even when he was right," comments Sibilla. "There was a wonderful wing chair he told me was so chic and elegant, but I wanted soft, cozy chairs then. Now I wish I *had* got that chair. And his work doesn't date at all the way modern rooms do. It's like a Balenciaga or Givenchy dress—good for-ever." But it takes two, I say. Sibilla is always astute and she *listens*. Everyone at Irvine & Fleming simply adores her—with good reason. Bella Sibilla! 🐾

Best in Show

THE KIPS BAY DECORATOR SHOW HOUSE in New York was one of the first decorator show houses and is still the most prestigious platform in the country for decorators and designers—though now America is awash in such charity projects. When show houses first appeared on the scene, Tom Fleming and I were wary of the idea. We were usually rather adverse to publicity—our jobs in those days came only through recommendations, and our clients were extremely private. But we were seduced into getting involved by a bunch of glamorous and very hardworking women who were the lifeforce behind the whole idea—especially Helen Hollerith, Rella McDougal, and Jane Poole. When we visited the Kips Bay Boys Club, (now the Kips Bay Boys & Girls Club, and located in the South Bronx since 1969), we were quickly impressed by the spirit and success of the well-run organization.

Stupendous Stairway

Irvine & Fleming first participated in the Kips Bay Show House in 1980. As newcomers, we were assigned a large stair landing rather than a major room. We put it together as a lounge hall—a bit of an anomaly, since visitors passed through the space in endless procession.

Two enormous rooms flanked our space, one decorated by Mark Hampton and the other by Robert Metzger. Mark's library was an instant classic. It had rich, dark, *dark* brown walls, staggering antiques and paintings, and a profusion of books that looked as if they had actually been read. The upholstered furniture was covered in that most American of fabrics, white cotton dimity. Mark was gentlemanly, if slightly reserved; we did not really know each other then. La

Opposite:
The focal point of the stair landing is an expanse of mirrored glass with an oval gilt Adam mirror and a constellation of French porcelain plates hanging on it. Beneath this composition is an enormously deep sofa covered in Hollyhock chintz with a Chinese yellow background.

We used decorators' tricks—
mirroring mirrors and dramatic
curtains in a tonal space—to open
up the long and narrow room.

Metzger, on the other hand, was coldly distant, and I don't think he ever actually spoke to me. His vast room was in the vanguard of the overrich, overworked, show-off media room—we still suffer from this horror. The day before the opening, his chauffeur came to pick him up for lunch. He emerged from his media room, paused a moment to observe us all hanging off ladders (after committing ourselves to the second-floor landing, we discovered that we were required to continue our elaborate paint job all the way down to the ground-floor hall), and said, "Well, they must have *something* in mind!" On opening night, the Irvine & Fleming crew had fun gazing down the curved staircase and speculating which of the two rooms visitors would pick as they glided though our landing.

During the run of the show, a longtime client with whom I had quarreled five years before left a note: "Brilliantly put together as usual. Loved the photograph of your mother as a VAD." It was signed "your ex-client Drue Heinz." Within a few months, we were working on the decoration of the Pittsburgh concert hall, Heinz Hall, and on the Heinzes' private jet—which she stipulated should look like Chanel's brown *salon* in Paris.

English Sitting Room

A year or two later, it was time for an encore. We got a room this time, but it was a difficult one—long, dark, and not very wide. We decided to develop it as a comfortable sitting room. To help divide the length, we built a false chimney breast in the middle of one wall and installed a beautiful eighteenth-century Scottish pine mantel. We mirrored the upper part of the chimney breast and installed a mirrored panel of the same width on the opposite wall—this will make a room seem wider. To lighten the feel of the space, we covered the walls in natural Japanese straw cloth outlined in natural

Chippy's portraits of daughter Jassy and dog Victoria in the bar/dressing room.

split bamboo. In the same natural vein, we covered the floor from wall to wall in the famous, costly, and still all hand-woven rush carpet made by the Waveney Apple Growers in Suffolk. Usually, it takes a year to fill an order, but my contacts at Colefax & Fowler helped me secure just enough already woven yardage for the room. By the way, it is true that it must be watered once a month in England and almost every three days in an overheated New York apartment.)

We covered a large sofa in straw-colored linen, and for the dressy curtains and a chair with ottoman, we used a vivid strawberry-colored Colefax & Fowler cotton print. This strong shot of color and pattern also helped to shorten the room. The rest of the space was an eclectic mix: a top-drawer Louis XVI *bergère,* covered in its original leather; and my client Leola MacDonald's eternal and time-worn painted wicker armchair (see page 211).

The curtains in the lavish bedroom are made of three tones of cream Roman satin with festoons of unlined cream linen. The bed is draped in the darkest cream satin; the strong French blue lining echoes the Plumbago chintz on the chair.

The walk-in closet we turned into an amusing bar and dressing room. The walls were papered in Fuchsia Arch, and the ceiling was faux-tented with a striped wallpaper divided by grosgrain ribbon. At the back, our younger daughter, Jassy, who was eight, and our beloved dog, Victoria, peered through a French door with polite white batiste curtains—Chippy had painted these portraits on the brown-tinted mirrored-glass door panels.

Grand Georgian "Bedsit"

In decorating show house rooms, I have always hung the idea for the design on one person. The supposed inspiration for this stylish bedroom was one of my favorite clients, Leola MacDonald. We had a large room, so we could accommodate the various furnishings needed in a couple's "holy of holies" private space: bed, desk, window seat, comfortable chairs, play and task table, and fireplace. To rein in the spaciousness of the room and give the eye a bit of a treat, I used my well-honed shadow-panel paint technique, which immediately provided a hint of Georgian refinement.

Elaborate, modern interpretations of Regency-style "London" curtains and bed hangings were made of rich deep cream silk and linen. The bed hangings were lined in solid Nattier blue—the French eighteenth-century painter so loved this color—to coordinate with the blue and cream Plumbago chintz (see page 287). The bed was angled as a slight eccentricity. The whole mix speaks of what I admire so much—the look of a true-and-tried room that has evolved and deepened in atmosphere over a period of time. I call my attempts at this design approach "instant accumulation"—rather like a literary, erudite film set.

French Neoclassical Studio

I worked on this sitting room with Sam Blount, who was then my assistant. It was an opportunity for Sam to get his feet wet and to get some personal credit, helped along by my

Photo albums and games sit atop a Regency pedestal table. A horsehair seat pad shaped to the bay window, covered in mattress ticking, and tufted with buttons is an idea copied from the eighteenth century.

savoir faire. Sam recently told Chippy, "I was fortunate to have worked with Keith for twelve years, first as his assistant, than as a partner. Learning the ropes with Keith was a lot like his work: his decorating talents are well known but he is also a gifted architect and landscape designer and not-so-frustrated actor. He is a master at decorative detailing and has an uncanny ability to observe and retain. He could point out Aunt Pittypat's stair hall wallpaper (one I still use) from *Gone with the Wind*, comment on the elaborate curtain details at Castle Howard, take note of the napkin trim on the Orient Express, admire the architecture of Monticello and the gardens at Vaux le Vicomte, as well as want to chop down every rhododendron in sight at Sudbury, Derbyshire. Keith taught me how important it is to observe with 'eyes wide open.' I apply this to my own business every day. Keith would often quote one of his favorite movie stars, Bette Davis: 'Fasten your seat belts. It's going to be a bumpy night.' Even with an occasional bump, I feel privileged to have known and worked with Keith, to have tapped into a portion of his generosity, historical knowledge, and endless creativity."

With this Kips Bay sitting room, the inspiration was one of my first American clients, Frances Leggett, well respected and, alas, long-since dead. She was a grand dame of the old American school, like Mrs. Lytle Hull or Alice Roosevelt Longworth, both friends of hers. Frances Leggett had a great penchant for neo-classical and Empire furniture; the memories of her predilections gave us the theme for the room. The trim and walls were painted in tones of pure white and ivory white, which complemented the French marble mantel already in the room. Then we gave the walls a paneled look with an unusual wallpaper border

A ticking slipcovered chair sits up to a writing table in the window (Nancy Lancaster's desk *encore*). One of my favorite tricks is a deep pink pleated silk lampshade on a simple Chinese vase lamp, which seems to look good in almost every room.

Opposite:
Many of the furnishings in the sitting room were purchased for clients on a London shopping trip just before the show house opened. The Regency black and gilt mirror with Greek key motif was on its way to Susan Rotenstreich. The black-lacquer antique four-tier whatnot would soon be off to Leola MacDonald in the Hamptons. And the pair of eighteenth-century black-lacquer chinoiserie pole firescreens were to be a housewarming present for Lucille and Geoffrey Berenson.

An odd assortment of cushions—some antique and some made from antique fabrics—on the slipcovered recamier. On the wall is a Botero nude above a Picasso dove plate.

in black, white, and tan. We reduced the height of the room by painting and glazing the ceiling and then punching the surface with bunched-up cotton muslin wads (or rags) for a ragged, open texture. The color was dark peacock green; painted around the edge was a Greek key border. This treatment gave the room an early-nineteenth-century French quality, harking back to a time when this kind of coloring and borders were *tout la rage*.

The floor was covered in practical sisal, and a white Arctic wolf pelt lay in front of the hearth. We went so far as to find an antique coal scuttle and, even more difficult, lumps of real coal to fill it. (I kept the coal; we have used it over the years for the Scottish New Year's custom of "first footing." It has also come in handy to smoke a bees' nest out of our chimney at St. Johns Farm.) Most of the overstuffed furniture was slipcovered in mattress ticking—the covers were purposefully loose and ill-fitting to ape the made-at-home ones run up by English nannies. (Ours were run up by Chippy, who had strict instructions to make the hems deliberately and obviously uneven!)

In her earlier life in England as Lady Margesson, Mrs. Leggett knew well the aristocratic quality of "intended imperfection." The wood furniture and *objets d'art* in the room were a mélange of classical pieces. One was an elegant recamier I had bought at ruinous expense from Colefax & Fowler for Leola MacDonald. Before it was upholstered, I had asked her to take a look at it in the workshop. She sat on it—and it immediately collapsed! The recamier was riddled with worms and had to be completely reconstructed. Since Leola is who she is, she was more amused than upset. As a final titillation in the room, we hung a Botero painting of an almost shockingly overweight nude.

Anglo-Saxon French Moderne

Our drawing room for Kips Bay in 2002 was designed primarily by my assistant, Jason Bell. He had the advantage of eager-to-learn artistic eyes, and in his six years with us, he became well honed as a traditionalist. Of his time at Irvine & Fleming, Jason says: "My experience with Keith was a roller coaster through the world of interior design. His spirit and style taught me never to be afraid of color or pattern. Keith has an ability to create beauty and timeless style from a blank palette."

The dramatic curtains in the drawing room were inspired by French door openings, and especially by the canopies outside the Ritz in the Place Vendôme, which Jason had seen on a Christmas trip to Paris. The walls of the plaster-paneled living room were softly glazed in a washed-out blue to focus on these unusual curtains. The rest of the room was closer to an Irvine & Fleming eclectic traditional mix—but filtered through a younger eye. One notable element was the fine faded old Tabriz rug. I have always loved rugs that are "silvered" with age—and look as though they might well be in their *last week!*

Felicity Wilde's design is an energetic and exciting reassessment of a traditional paneled room.

On the wall behind the piano in the dining/music room are silhouettes of Chippy and me.

Vogue Regency for the Millennium

For our 2005 room at Kips Bay—a large paneled area on the ground floor of a grand house—I let my assistant, Felicity Wilde, run with ideas—and she did not disappoint. She decided to make the dining/music room an homage to my style of decorating. (I'm reminded of Karl Lagerfeld's brilliant take on Chanel and also of Burberry's early-twenty-first-century.) I have collected antique silhouettes for years, so Felicity had some of my favorites—including two modern ones of Chippy and me—blown up to enormous size by the California artist Karl Johnson. Black and gilt frames were equally massive. Then—heavens!—she hung them on walls glazed in a vivid Granny-Smith-green.

There were precedents for everything in the room, but the effect was modern and eclectic. Portraits on dining room walls, for example, are a grand European tradition. The daring green recalls Elsa Schiaparelli's shocking pink as well as Charles Beistegui's bold use of color. Adding to the graphic and rather 1930s Liquorice Allsorts quality were black and white striped silk curtains, which were chosen for the dressmaker look of the fabric and also for the eccentric Brighton Pavilion style.

The floor was painted in a classical Federal design of octagons with a Greek key border, and Felicity banned my usual tendency toward clutter. A grand piano occupied one corner of the room; Chippy supplied a copy of Noel Coward's "London Pride," with a lime green cover from her trove of sheet music. A double bass and music stand rested in another corner, and a games table sat in a third. The eclectic furniture was chosen for crisp line, color, and quality, rather than period. There were two exemplary 1810 Baltic commodes, French modernist lamps from the 1940s, Philippe Starck's Louis Ghost chairs, decorative accessories from the 1930s to the 1950s, a huge French rustic clock face, and two ancient Greek bronze heads borrowed from our house. A dining table for eight

The table, sixty-four inches square, seats eight people in a way that they can talk to each other easily. Made from plywood, it is covered with a black velvet cloth.

sat bang in the middle. Visitors had a good time reading the names on the place cards. How smart the room was! What fun it would have been to have a dinner party there!

By now, we are accustomed to these client-free show houses, which garner meaningful amounts of money for the sponsoring charities. Tom Fleming has done many rooms in the summer Hampton Designer Showhouse in Southampton. We have done tables for Tiffany's, room vignettes for the Mount Vernon Hotel Museum & Garden (formerly the Abigail Adams Smith Museum in New York), show houses in Washington, D.C., and Greenwich, Connecticut, and even designer Christmas trees. The show house must go on. 🐱

A House in the Hamptons

Mark Hampton's watercolor of the MacDonalds' house.

I FIRST MET Leola and Robbie MacDonald in 1962. Leola had been a college classmate of Susie Sloane, my first dazzling girl assistant. The MacDonalds, only recently married, had bought an old brownstone way up in the high nineties on the East Side of Manhattan—it seemed not only eccentric but almost at the frontier.

An architect friend of theirs restored and renovated the house. The old brownstone room allocation was broken down and re-formed as an "open plan"—after all, it was the early 1960s! I instinctively knew that this was a gimmicky, passing phase—the result is a house with no serious separation or privacy, and all sorts of problems for the interior design. Nevertheless, gradually over the next three decades, the MacDonalds' brownstone evolved into a house full of character and comfort.

As a bonus for our efforts, in the early 1970s, Leola and Robbie bought a charming white clapboard house in the Hamptons. The late Mark Hampton, a great family friend, did one of his charming watercolors of the exterior. I often wondered why Leola did not turn to Mark to help with her houses. "Why would I desert Keith?" she asked Chippy. "The great thing about him is that he never tells you to throw anything out, or urges you to do things over. Some of my pillows have faded in the sun, but he says they're fine. A friend told me I have the best-looking pillows! Keith may occasionally try some semi-bullying, but in the end, he is always right. It can be quite irritating!"

We kept the design components inside the house extremely cottage-y—but assuredly Colefax & Fowler cottage-y! And we inflected it toward these particular clients: the MacDonalds are witty, bright, and literary, so we played lots of intellectual games by juxtaposing unusual elements.

Opposite:
A screen of two antique pine columns and two pilasters made to match improves the flow between drawing room and dining room; it also makes a festive entrance to the latter. The mattress-ticking slipcover on the Regency recamier—held over from a Kips Bay showhouse—keeps the room from becoming too formal.

209

The bow-fronted Hepplewhite settee contributes a sense of increased volume to the long, narrow entrance hall, as does the wallpaper, which reaches up to the second floor. The insides of the shelves were painted blue to blend with the door paneling and a skirted table.

The entrance hall, long but quite narrow, gives the impression of being larger than it is. I found an unusual wallpaper with a toile pattern depicting American birds (*hélas,* a discontinued Winterthur documentary design) to wrap the space and sweep up the staircase to the second floor. A mellow old Sultanabad rug softened the wood floor, and a lovely, slightly bowfront Hepplewhite settee covered in an English Regency–style cotton print invited comfy collapse. Dark blue paint striping on the trim and doors echoed the blue cotton print of a skirted table and accentuated the "grand" cottage feel.

The drawing room was warm and vibrant, with drag-glazed coral walls highlighted by Lady Colefax–inspired, striped, coral and cream "Vogue Regency" curtains—pure England in the 1930s. (I recently saw the Sibyl Colefax rooms at the Angleseys' great Plas Newydd in Wales—old Sibyl was no

Curtains in the drawing room were inspired by Sibyl Colefax. Osbert Lancaster, that eagle-eyed cartoonist and observer of houses and interiors, would have dubbed them "Vogue Regency."

mean slouch as a decorator!) Most of the overstuffed furniture in the room as well as the sofalike banquette in the bay window was covered in my favorite hand-blocked English chintz, Trenton Hall. How livable it always is! By contrast, stony-beige linen damask upholstered beautiful antique French fruitwood *bergère* chairs. Mattress ticking (the same as on page 202) slipcovered an exemplary black-lacquer Regency settee, adding insouciance to its chic shape and bumping it down just a little. Beside the settee was a poor but lovable relation—an Edwardian wicker chair, beat-up yet comfortable, its timeworn paint epitomizing John Fowler's well-known (but not original) phrase "pleasing decay." It cost forty-five dollars in the 1960s and has been in every MacDonald abode (and once I even borrowed it for a room at the Kips Bay Boys Club Showhouse in New York; see page 197). Since then, the wicker chair with the

Blue glassware on the table in the dining room picks up the soft and strong blues of the painted paneling on the walls.

nearest *au point* beat-up look to it I have come across cost three thousand dollars!

We decided to knock down the wall between the drawing room and the dining room. This large opening, with a screen of columns and pilasters (the pilasters were new, made to match the antique pine columns I had found), made movement flow more comfortably during relaxed summer weekends. Mark Hampton, a frequent visitor, liked the idea so much he knocked it off (with my permission) in his Park Avenue apartment.

The dining room was pure Colefax & Fowler from its washed-out blue shadow-paneled walls to its dressy English country influence. Shadow-paneling is a paint technique developed in Georgian England; it simulates panels where real wood panels would have been too expensive. Larger "panels" (all on a flat surface, of course) are glazed in a lighter tone than "stiles" and "rails." Thin pencil lines between the two shades—lighter on one side and darker on the other—produce an illusion of depth and shadow. In a world of English reverse snobbery, shadow-paneling became smarter than the real thing—how typical! The technique was a great favorite of John Fowler's—in fact, he rediscovered it—and I have delighted in its use for decades.

The paneled walls were perfect for arrangements of Leola's large collection of Liverpool Transfer plates, with their finely drawn exotic birds, and an assortment of deer antlers (MacDonald *is* a Scottish name!). The soft blue varied background was played off against blue and white English Leaf Stripe chintz curtains. A gilt and ebony Regency convex bull's-eye mirror enjoyed pride of place above the mantel, reflecting the drawing room beyond. My favorite pieces in the room were the unmatched Chippendale chairs—no two alike—that marched around the table. Forget Mallett's and the Grosvenor House

Reflected in the convex mirror of the dining room is the screen of pine columns and pilasters, and then the red-curtained drawing room.

antique fair and that whole world of overworked show-off Georgian furniture. These sturdy, simple chairs speak volumes about the *real* eighteenth-century English style of life. These were the chairs that Hogarth, Dr. Johnson, and David Garrick lived with. Now they are costly and hard as hens' teeth to find. My heart turns cartwheels whenever I come across one.

The breakfast room/kitchen was much simpler, more family-oriented with its terra-cotta tile floor and rough plastered walls outlined by green Portuguese ceramic tiles. The tiles were not simply stuck onto the walls; the plaster was built out so that tiles and wall formed the same smooth surface. The antique French farm table, oak Windsor chairs, and slightly unexpected leather wing chair were comfortable and inviting and seemed happily connected with the rolling lawn, overscaled hedges, and great trees outside. 🐾

Country Cottage in Town

Dick Rich is Brooklyn born and bred; he was one of the all-time greats in the competitive world of American advertising. He was a founder of Wells Rich Greene and the creative genius behind such legendary ad campaigns as Alka-Seltzer's "No matter what shape your stomach's in" and Benson & Hedges' witty visuals. Dick's wife, Silvia, is an Italian-American with a classic Nordic look, eternally blond and statuesque; she is an enthusiastic *hausfrau* and gardener, records books for the blind, cleans the streets, and is an admired eccentric.

I first met the Riches in the 1960s when I designed two floors in the then newly built General Motors Building for the flushed-with-success Wells Rich Greene (see pages 33–35). At about the same time, Dick bought a large town house in the east sixties in Manhattan and retained me as the interior designer. Dick and Silvia spent almost four happy decades raising their family in this house.

In 2002, Dick telephoned the Irvine & Fleming office and asked, "Are any of them still alive?" When told "they" were, he deadpanned, "Tell Keith he did my house thirty-five years ago, and I have a complaint." With the family flown the coop and mostly married off, the Riches had traded the large house—traditional and a trifle grand—for a smaller, more compact house slightly farther north. The couple desired more relaxed surroundings, almost a country house in the heart of Manhattan. The house had been split up into flats by previous owners, so a great deal of space planning and some construction was necessary before we could really get started. We worked with one of my well-tried New York contractors, Steve Godwin. Then my assistant, Felicity Wilde, and I began to work with the pleasing abundance of furniture and antiques that were ready for a new home and a fresh lease on life.

Opposite:
Straw Madagascar cloth walls provide the backdrop for the Riches' dining room area. The Chinese rug—and even the floorboards—are all faux-painted. The cane-backed chairs with wool-tartan-covered seat pads have a casual, country look that counteracts the sophistication of the painted rug.

We tried to make the large family-living-dining room comfortable and well-suited to the Riches' new way of life. Some exposed brick walls—so desirable in the 1950s and 1960s, but very West Village and definitely no longer for *our* age group—were sheetrocked; next, we lined the whole space in natural straw Madagascar cloth, always serene and dateless and an appropriate backdrop for art as well. The large area, which wrapped around one of those dratted recessed plasma televisions, was informal and unintimidating. The upholstery in the living area was a mélange of blues—solid, striped, checked, and patterned (on the pillows). Two important family members, Stan and Ollie—a beagle and an English bulldog, neither entirely house-trained—led to our most astute design decision. We could not entertain the idea of real antique rugs, so we decided to faux-paint them on a floor itself faux-painted to resemble planks of bleached pine. I borrowed two antique Chinese rugs in tones of blue and beige; these were meticulously copied in paint—including ripples, tiny imperfections, uneven edges, and skew-whiff crumpled fringes—one centered in the living area and the other under the table in the dining area. They are vastly amusing and give a personal character to the space. So convincing were they that Tom Fleming, on entering the room, exclaimed, "Where did you find those great rugs?"

The library was dominated by solid-white-oak architectural bookcases pickled to give a creamy, bleached effect that still retained the beauty of the grain (a technique made famous by decorator Syrie Maugham in the 1920s and 1930s). The backs of the bookcase interiors were glazed in red to give drama and depth, a favorite effect of mine. Echoing the neutral palette of the bookcases, the walls were papered in a historic Owen Jones design of soft putty tones—Jones was the great late-nineteenth-century designer of patterns for the architect A. W. N. Pugin, among others. This muted masculine background was emboldened by a large sofa upholstered in a punchy ikat-inspired print in brown, beige, and Indian red. An unusual brown-toned wool Glencoe tartan covered two overstuffed armchairs with matching ottomans. The carpeting was the always chic but eminently practical ocelot design.

The master bedroom, which had been reconfigured into a rather large space during the construction, looked out over garden and trees—a view that seemed to hint at a remote northern Connecticut rather than at Manhattan. Walls, window

Opposite:
A painting suggests a key to the colors used in the library area.

217

Fabric on frame chairs in the master bedroom is Colefax & Fowler's Pink Oakleaf. The carpet has a wall-to-wall trellis pattern.

curtains, and sofa were romantically swathed in Pillement, a linen chinoiserie toile de Jouy. Inside the hangings on the oak canopy bed was Fancy, a dainty green-on-cream Colefax & Fowler glazed chintz. Simple printed patterns of this type were often used to line curtains in the early nineteenth century, and these linings would have been visible from the exterior of the house. In this vein, we lined curtains in both the library upstairs and the living room below in outrageous colors—royal blue and scarlet—just to wake up the neighborhood. (The interlinings were off-white, naturally.)

A glass French door led to the Riches' newly enlarged bathroom, a dream-like haven of calm and peace. Its unpretentious *faux-marbre* floor—warmer and much wittier than real marble—and glazed and striped trim and cabinetry were complemented by delicate, neutral, sprigged wallpaper. The deeply recessed window behind the bathtub was mirrored on both sides, an old trick that increases the quantity of light in a room. In the basement was a complete guest suite for friends and family as well as a light-hearted laundry. Felicity worked out the plumbing so that the cold pipes were painted blue and the hot pipes red. The Riches, ensconced in their Manhattan country cottage with its pretty garden, were soon as happy as bugs in a faux Chinese rug. 🐱

The mirror over the vanity reflects the garden window and a French door to the master bedroom.

Gorgeous Georgian

DEBBIE AND PHILIPPE DAUMAN are an international couple—she is American, he French. A pretty, ethereal blond, Debbie belies her fragile looks with serious efficiency and organization. Philippe, who has loads of Gallic charm, is a business panjandrum. Both are thoroughly social Manhattanites who in 1987 bought a handsome double town house on the Upper East Side.

When Debbie and Phillipe first approached me to decorate the house, they had already interviewed many interior designers, including some of my major competitors, and they were still undecided. Debbie had excellent and enthusiastic natural taste, and she had decorated their house in East Hampton and their previous apartment in New York, just a few blocks away, on her own. However, both she and Philippe realized this major house required serious professional help. "I told him it was a *big* house, and Keith answered, 'We've done big houses before,'" Debbie recently told Chippy. When she and I first sat down together, she showed me, in her organized way, a portfolio of magazine clippings she really liked. A clever opening move, I thought, amused—and pleased—to see that half the shots were of Irvine & Fleming work, and another quarter were Colefax & Fowler. It was compatibility in one instant. Through the next long year of construction, restoration, and decoration, Debbie listened attentively to every one of my ideas and suggestions. She continually repeated, "One doesn't go to a decorator of your caliber and *not* listen and learn."

The house was tired and worn. It had fairly good Georgian-style details but lacked color and spirit. In fact, it was what we in England have dubbed Bankers' Georgian, a name conjured by the puissant architectural observer and caricaturist Sir Osbert Lancaster to imply boring but well-heeled respectability. The town

This great marble bust of Louis XIV (with a broken nose) was found in Norwich, England—Debbie and I fought over it, and she won!

Opposite:
Under the spectacular staircase is a hall table skirted in Harrow Damask, a documentary chintz I found in London and gave to Brunschwig & Fils. For some years, it was the company's top-selling fabric.

221

Architectural broken pediments dramatize the doorways of the enfilade of rooms on the piano nobile. They lead from the green-glazed dining room with its scenic-paper-covered screens across the landing to the elegant lemon yellow drawing room. On the landing is an amorphous English Regency table.

house was in reasonably good shape—only three families had resided there since it was built in 1918—so the difficulty lay in fitting new systems into an old structure without compromising its integrity and style. "Any good decorator could have done it in a straightforward, conventional way," said Debbie, "but Keith brought to each room a certain unexpected magic."

The imposing hall was already distinguished by a graphic black and white marble floor in need of little repair. This surefire effect *always* works. Here, it led to an impressive Adamesque staircase circling a filigreed plaster dome designed by me and installed by a master plasterer. Ionic columns divided the hall into three sections; the walls of each section were glazed with varying intensities of coral. The central part of the hall was lined above the paneled dado with John Fowler's famous hand-blocked wallpaper Pembroke Damask. Fowler had discovered old fragments of this paper at Wilton House in Wiltshire when he was working there for the Earl of Pembroke, and he prevailed on the wallpaper company Coles to cut new blocks for it. As far as I know, it is the most expensive wallpaper in the world—but probably not! This paper also sweeps up the wall by the staircase to the piano nobile, which boasted a distinguished enfilade of superb rooms for entertaining. The exquisite drawing room, dignified library, and dramatic dining room were connected by overscaled dog-eared classical doorways topped with broken pediments.

In the drawing room, I used a favorite Fowler technique that imitates early Georgian painted rooms, shadow-glazing panels in two tones of yellow accented with tiny dark and light lines. The lemony palette continued in the elegant "London" swagged curtains, which were made from three shades of silk taffeta trimmed with braid (to define the edges), corded rosettes, and tassels on cords. A Sheraton settee was upholstered with a subtle yellow-on-cream toile de Jouy, a nearby armchair in a floral glazed chintz. All this herbaceous-border-colored exuberance was enhanced by a flawless moss green floral Aubusson rug of about

1800. I loathe Aubussons made in the last half of the nineteenth century—even though since about 1970 they have frequently been considered the *most* desirable rugs. Only Napoleonic Empire ones will do for me!

The paneled dining room was glazed in four different tones of green, all highlighted with a thin, dark pomegranate line. Tall wing chairs around the table were upholstered in the grand-scaled chintz Le Lac. These chairs could be supplemented by a distinguished set of eight painted Hepplewhite chairs that came

The atmosphere in the drawing room was achieved by setting flowery colors and patterns against delicate lemon-sherbet-glazed walls and silk-satin curtains. A pretty painted Adam settee is covered in a yellow and white toile found in London; above is an Adam gilt and gesso mirror surrounded by silhouettes and miniatures.

Refined strié paintwork in several shades of green adds depth and interest to the mantelpiece in the dining room. The overmantel frames an outsized Regency bull's-eye mirror. On the mantel shelf are antique Delft vases and pots in the Chinese style.

from Cumbria, in the north of England, where they had been sitting since the eighteenth century. One early morning, on a sortie looking for antiques, I bought them straight from the delivery van just before they were to be taken into the London shop of the late, great antique dealer O. F. (Jack) Wilson. We needed ten to complete the dining room, and so Wilson made up two reproductions—so exquisitely that even *I* can hardly tell them from the real ones. Alternating upholstered and more conventional dining chairs around a table—a trick Nancy Lancaster always used— is charmingly inviting if a bit idiosyncratic. The dining room was anchored by the lively Colefax & Fowler Rocksavage patterned wool rug, and in each corner stood one of four tall screens made from an early-nineteenth-century French grisaille scenic paper by Zuber.

The vast library had the scale and presence of a great old English room, an exclusive gentleman's club perhaps. Warm solid-oak panels were complemented by an overscaled burnt orange linen print from England; Thames green curtains with braid-trimmed valences provided some contrast, and a vibrant antique Bukhara rug provided some emphasis. Despite its masculinity, the room made women look great, and they felt comfortable there. I have often observed that women feel most at home in rooms created specially for men.

Off the library was a snug, denlike telephone room. When I was first in this business, all grand houses had a telephone room. It was most impolite to talk on the telephone in front of guests, or even family. With its eighteenth-century pine paneling and the superbly drawn French toile La Dame du Lac upholstering a William IV armchair, the room was a hideaway not only for a telephone call but for a private talk or drink. (On the subject of telephone rooms, Katharine Graham's mother, Mrs. Eugene Meyer, had a fabulous one off the front hall of her Washington mansion. She would descend the staircase for lunch, dressed in a long skirt and carrying a cane, at exactly one o'clock and would join Mrs. Graham and myself in the telephone room for a quick aperitif. The room was comfortable and very dated, and the furniture was centered around a low coffee table holding an old-fashioned upright telephone with a speaking trumpet. Mrs. Meyer always reminded us that on this telephone she would call President Truman and say, "Harry, I don't agree with what you're doing!")

Upstairs, the pièce de résistance was the romantic, seriously feminine master bedroom. A master bedroom, the woman's nerve center of the house, should always be feminine. But as I told Suzanne Slesin for an article she wrote about the Daumans' house for *House & Garden*, "Women hesitate to emphasize the feminine for fear their husbands will be

A Georgian-style plaster ceiling adds light to the oak-paneled library. At the end of the room is a large-scale Irish console with a marble top. Over it is a pair of fine George II gilt mirrors with candle arms. The room has plenty of easy furniture covered in a mix of patterns.

unhappy. However, my experience shows that usually you can persuade a husband faster than a wife." In this case, Debbie was in charge from the start. She rarely showed Philippe the decorating plans because, she says, "Keith doesn't always do the safe thing, and it needs to be seen finished to be able to see how it works. So I told Philippe he'd see it when it was done. And he was thrilled."

The pink lining of the bed hangings makes this bedroom ultra-feminine. The diminutive settee at the foot of the bed is covered with a French toile called Les Enfants.

Philippe's bathroom was paneled and then faux-painted to resemble rosewood, making a tiny French Empire fantasy that combined a French toile, Coronation of Napoleon, with a painted-tole Napoleonic cocked-hat light fixture. After all, Philippe Dauman is French—and an executive alpha male! In contrast, Debbie's dainty bathroom, lined with watercolor paneling in floral motifs (painted by Dynaflow Studios in Brooklyn, New York), was inspired by early-twentieth-century children's book paintings by the Dutch illustrator Henriette Willebeek Le Mair. These charming oval-shaped scenes, bordered with leaves and flowers, depict impeccably dressed, good-as-gold children in ideal gardens and interiors—just what any parent (impossibly) aches for!

The town house has proved eminently practical. Younger son Alexandre, still living at home, has stated—as once we all would have—that when he leaves, he wants a *small* flat and a *dog!* The house has also attained the feeling of permanence characteristic of the great, mellow residences of London and Paris—with none of the jittery search for change that affects many American interiors. It is a now-and-future family house, steered and commanded by "General" Debbie Dauman. 🐾

The custom-colored wall-to-wall carpet in the master bedroom harmonizes with the blue-glazed and -strié-painted walls and woodwork.

Iconic Mother and Myth

WHY DID I REALLY come to America? The honest answer goes back to around 1956. Colefax & Fowler was redoing Boughton House in Northamptonshire, the English seat of the Duke and Duchess of Buccleuch, an estate known as the English Versailles. Then Fowler's assistant, I took the train up one day before him to note and measure certain situations. I arrived late in the evening (I am sure I had to work at Brook Street until five o'clock), and a footman led me to a cozy little bedroom up under the leads; a delicious supper was laid out before the fire in an adjoining sitting room. The next morning, awakened by the rooks cawing in the park, I quickly shaved and dressed. No one had told me when or where to appear, so girding my courage, I sallied forth. I descended one staircase, then one on a larger scale, and then one even more imposing, this time leading to seriously grand Piranesian vistas. Pausing indecisively, I suddenly glimpsed a golden Labrador cross the hall, seemingly miles away. I followed the retriever to a charming breakfast room where Her Grace was at her post. She was delightful and easy and, after I had eaten, showed me where to get to work on my chores.

Late in the morning, Mr. Fowler arrived, and I was fast made wise that everything I had put together so far was "quite wrong." I reworked it for an hour or so and then started downstairs. The duchess and Mr. Fowler were in the hall below, and as I reached the landing, the duchess said, "John, should I ask Mr. . . . Mr. . . . Erwin? . . . to lunch?" Fowler said, "Oh, he can just eat with the servants." If it had happened today, I would have yelled, "I'm outta here!"

A year and a half later, I was in New York, working for Mrs. Henry Parish II and already unhappy—even though it had only been three weeks. On a day trip to Washington, D.C., to visit Mrs. John Sherman Cooper (the former Lorraine

Opposite:
The living room of Mrs. Kennedy's New York apartment reflects the quiet European elegance she gradually embraced.

In the library, classic draped curtains and a buttoned slipper chair play off against a sofa slipcovered in an African print.

Rowan), an almost identical scenario arose. Dazzling, witty, and cultivated, Mrs. Cooper (later to become one of my most admired clients) asked Sister P., "Should Mr. Irvine lunch with us?" (She was American, and so she remembered my name.) Sister said, "He can just run out and get a hamburger." Mrs. Cooper came right up to me and said, "Of course you will have lunch with us." Oh, I came to the *right* democratic country! And what a lunch it was! I was seated between Jacqueline Kennedy and Mme. Pandit Nehru. Also at the table was Evangeline Bruce; Joe Alsop and Bill Walton were catnip for the ladies. I had been in America such a short time—what a difference a day makes.

So it was thanks to the snobbery of the English that I came to work for America's great democratic family. For after the luncheon, Mrs. Parish abandoned me: she had sniffed out a possible rich client in Virginia. I had no money and no airplane ticket, but something even better: Mrs. Kennedy asked me to her house on N Street to look at some things she had done. She cleverly put me at my ease, making me feel as though I knew much more than she did—an encouraging and ego-massaging idea. She drove me to the airport and lent me money for the ticket (the brand-new shuttle was just fourteen dollars in those golden days) and a taxi home. Within nine months, I had left Sister, and the Kennedys, the Coopers, and Mrs. Earl E. T. Smith in New York had come to me as clients. They were all great recommenders—the yeast of the decorating business. Indeed, this triumvirate really started my whole career.

I did odds and ends for the Kennedys during JFK's run for the presidency, but once he was elected I was passed over—after all, I was not an American. (Back then, no one had a clue that Stéphane Boudin was a behind-the-scenes advisor and that our first lady was running up vast bills at Jansen in Paris.) After the tragedy of the assassination, Jackie moved temporarily into the Averell Harrimans' Georgetown house, which I had just completed. A few months later, she bought a big house across the road and asked Billy Baldwin to help decorate it. Within six months, however, the media and the intrusive public—the tour buses on N Street almost closed Georgetown down—and their effect on her children drove Jackie crazy, so she up and moved to the more available anonymity of New York. She started working on her new apartment with Elizabeth Draper, a greatly underrated classic decorator (the Nancy Pierrepont of the 1950s and 1960s), and then, three years later, she contacted me again. Jackie asked me to do her bedroom, modeling it almost exactly on Marie Harriman's bedroom in

The much-disputed "too expensive" French linen brocade sofa.

231

Characteristic of Jackie's taste are fine French furniture, ravishing old master drawings, and classical sculpture.

Washington. Soon we added the library, living room, dining room, and children's rooms.

Concurrently, she lured me to her house in the Kennedy compound in Hyannis Port. It was rather forsaken—in fact, almost abandoned during the White House years—but we brightened and cheered it with South of France–inspired American and French cotton prints. The fabrics, primary colors on clean white backgrounds, came from Margowan, Woodson, Suzanne Fontan, and D. D. and Leslie Tillett. It was here in Hyannis Port that Mrs. Kennedy undertook her endless push for a special discount. But I held my ground, and the start was delayed for a few months. Finally, Nancy Tuckerman, Mrs. Kennedy's lifelong friend and super secretary, called and said, "Go ahead now!"

Round about this time, Mrs. Kennedy and Robert Kennedy were involved in a jobs project in Bedford-Stuyvesant, Brooklyn, then a center of disaffection and violence. A factory was set up in a restored commercial building to print fabrics based on traditional African designs. Jackie asked Leslie Tillett and me to help push it forward. So we made slipcovers, table skirts, and napkins in various designs for her apartment, and she allowed *House Beautiful* to publish them. However, they did not hang around long once their public relations value was proven!

Over the years, as Jackie grew more comfortable in her own skin, her taste deepened from Southampton/Alexandria/Kennedy 1960s pink-and-greenery all the way to dignified classicism with a decided preference for French taste (she was a Bouvier, after all). She liked top-quality painted and carved wood *boiserie* paneling, refined *ébéniste* Louis XV and Louis XVI furniture, deep *ton-sur-ton* color schemes, and unusual personal art. She is the only person I ever worked for who had twelve envy-inspiring Fuseli drawings. As she moved along this ever intensifying path, we began to change the living room of the Fifth Avenue apartment. We selected a subtle, expensive French linen for the largest sofa. As usual, we went through our game of discounts and "special" prices, so decisions were delayed. Then one morning, I glanced through the *Daily News* and there she was on Skorpios, marrying Aristotle Onassis. When Nancy Tuckerman called (again!) to say, "Go ahead," this time I asked, "Where do the bills go?" She said, "Oh, send them to Olympic Airlines."

Soon, though, Billy Baldwin was front and center on Skorpios. Yet I was constantly asked for my "input." Nancy would call early in the morning with that day's wish list. (I later learned that the Baldwin office received the same list.) We would rush around New York, and whoever came up with the best—and cheapest— version by midafternoon had to get it to Kennedy Airport for the Olympic flight to Athens. If the day's haul was considerable, the flight crew would have to remove seats and bump passengers. Mr. Onassis was not happy with Jackie's decorating efforts, and gradually she too lost interest, spending less and less time in Greece.

I observed over the years, as I withstood Mrs. Onassis's endless quest for a bargain, that as a rule she preferred working with my various assistants, though she always deferred to me on major decisions. Perhaps she thought that anything organized through an assistant would be less expensive. (In fact, everyone pays the same prices.) She adored Lee Barrett; and she enjoyed working with Richard Keith Langham when he was at Irvine & Fleming.

Our last project for Mrs. Onassis was a tiny lodge on the Mellon estate in Upperville, Virginia, where she kept her horses. (She hunted until late in her life.) Richard and I worked together on this simple little cottage, and Jackie always referred to it as "the chicken coop."

I truly loved my drifting times of contact with her, really a run of thirty-five years. From "queen of the world" to dedicated, caring mother, she was eternally erudite, naughtily witty, and beautifully mannered—a rare quality in our over-busy world. I do wish I could live until her diaries are someday published; I used to see them stacked in a corner of her bedroom and longed to take a peek. Jacqueline Kennedy Onassis was always a star at Irvine & Fleming, a towering figure of the twentieth century. 🐾

Mrs. Kennedy always had a drawing board in her living room because she loved sending letters illustrated with watercolors.

Connecticut Gold Coast

The William F. Buckleys (Bill and Pat, "the chic and stunning Mrs. Buckley," as *Women's Wear Daily* noted from time to time) were first referred to us in the 1970s by Rocky Converse (previously Gary Cooper's wife). The Buckleys were a marvelously amusing couple—he erudite, acerbic, and quick on the draw (just remember *Firing Line,* his controversial but galvanizing television program that, shockingly, bucked the liberal climate of the 1960s); she tall, elegant, and fascinating—a stand-up comic par excellence and a standout in any crowd.

Our first endeavor was the library in their apartment on the Upper East Side of Manhattan. Lacquered red almost out of existence, the room was also awash in deep red Fortuny damask. The odds and ends were meshed together by a dominating portrait of Pat in a bright pink Halston caftan, by the Englishman John Norton, that hung over the French Provençal (as a private joke, she always called it "French Pro-vin-ski-al") mantel.

We helped with a few other areas of the Manhattan maisonette, most of all in the entrance hall, but in the early 1970s, we were gradually enlisted to work with them on a midlife revamping of their lovely waterside house on the Connecticut side of Long Island Sound. Bill Buckley had a passion for building and alterations; Pat, on the other hand, declared it would be the death of her. Bill was "off on a toot" to add a music room; he was and is addicted to music. He also wanted to add an underground lap pool, a proposal that involved extending the outside terrace. The construction was a nightmare, but it produced marvelous results and added a much-used outdoor room. Pat and her serious green fingers soon had it draped in lantana, hibiscus, tea roses, and clematis.

Opposite:
In the sunroom, even the lamps have batik shades. The table holds photographs and a drawing of Bill Buckley.

Throughout the course of the project, we were treated to inspired marital bantering thoroughly enjoyed by both of them. Each had cultivated verbal gifts of timing and theatrical overemphasis. It was as good as—no, better than—a "Pat and Mike" Hepburn/Tracy movie. Bill would say, "Ducky, you will *love* it finished!" (He always called her Ducky.)

Bill's music room was the main thing. It was to house his newly acquired harpsichord, a lovely black and red instrument from Eric Herz of Boston. It played off well against walls treated to eight layers of scarlet lacquer (which proved rather difficult as we tried to hang Mr. Buckley's paintings). The ceiling was anaglypta molding, stapled, spackled, painted, and glazed to look like a real Jacobean plaster ceiling. The endless custom-made, curving, sectional sofa—the largest I know of in captivity—was covered in a multicolored English linen print, also Jacobean in inspiration (it was based on old crewel embroidery motifs). The sofa snaked its way through the room; as Pat quipped, "He has it like that so if he's playing, no one can escape." On the floor was the dark brown ocelot-patterned carpeting made famous by Elsie de Wolfe.

The Buckleys' dining room, which had previously been hung in a rather dated 1950s Parisian scenic wallpaper, complete with Eiffel Tower and poodles, was transformed into a psychedelic maelstrom of flaming orange walls, mauve crown molding, painted blue floor with black stripes, and pink patterned chairs. Pat simply loved color and being "with it," especially if it shook up other people.

The room that seemed to fit Mrs. Buckley's personality best was the sunroom. Its recessed window bay became an Edwardian-style Turkish corner complete with cushioned divan. The draped tented ceiling, curtains, and upholstered furnishings made use of at least forty Indonesian hand-blocked batik sarongs, some of which I brought back myself from a trip to Bali. The designers of those years—me included—were fascinated by batiks, especially after the opening of the shop China Seas in New York.

A master bedroom was constructed over the new terrace. Two of the corner walls were glass, so that the sweep of the sound was the main decoration. Pat asked us to cover the solid walls in soft beige ultrasuede—these being the Halston ultrasuede years, after all. It was around this time that Mrs. Buckley began to work more closely with Tom's talented assistant, Richard Keith Langham. (Chippy reminds me that he was *not* called Keith in our office, even though he had previously been known as Keith rather than as Richard!) I think, when the chips were down, that Tom and I were just a little too square for Mrs. Buckley. We generally avoided mixing socially with our illustrious clients, though we were often invited to do so. Richard, with his winning ways and southern charm, was much more Pat's *tasse de thé*.

For us, it was a disappointment. In my long career, losing both Katharine Graham and Pat Buckley has been a cloud of regret that never seems to blow away. But it was good for Richard Keith Langham, who recently reminisced with Chippy: "As an upstart from Alabama, I was wide-eyed to see how Keith conceived rooms with masterful nonchalance. His articulate detailing, furniture and pattern mixes, and exuberant color came out with a quiet genius. Keith cele-

French doors lead from the sunroom to the terrace and the view of Long Island Sound. In the foreground, Pat Buckley sits in the doorway in a peacock green Halston caftan, surrounded by the Buckleys' King Charles spaniels. I am reading in the distance.

brated talent in his underlings, introducing and promoting me to his harem of great ladies—Pat Buckley, Priscilla Rea, Drue Heinz, Jacqueline Onassis. He could mimic a southern drawl that would put mine to shame. After many an elaborate and exhausting installation, Keith would rush in and deliver his line from *Gone with the Wind:* 'We sho' is rich now!' My career was indeed made richer by all that I learned from him."

The rooms we helped with changed over the years, and a bad fire in the 1990s damaged the house. Thank goodness some photographs survived to record what I now think of as a period piece.

Connecticut Manor House

D<small>R</small>. J<small>AMES</small> R<small>EIBEL</small> and his wife, Barbara, tracked me down in the 1980s on the recommendation of a friend. I believe they were toying with the idea of working with Mark Hampton (our clients quite often seemed to overlap), but Barbara was not happy with the idea because another friend of hers was using him. However, after a two-hour meeting with them at their house, the job was in my pocket. I had mentally estimated the likely time and cost. Sitting on their patio in the watery early spring sunlight, Jay announced, "Okay, one year and one million dollars—but not a minute or a penny more." As it happened, we pulled the house together in a shorter time frame, and for less money.

I worked on the job with my assistant, Edwin Jackson; in fact, I think it was his first project with me. Except for some required structural additions and changes, our intention was to try to reuse everything from the Reibels' previous house in New Canaan, Connecticut, adding specific pieces only where there were gaps in the overall interior design plan.

The house itself was solid as a rock. It had been designed by John Russell Pope, the architect of the Jefferson Memorial and the National Gallery of Art, and so it was a "serious" house. The style was the same respectable Bankers' Georgian as Debbie and Philippe Dauman's town house in Manhattan. It was built in 1916, long before the Wall Street crash, and so construction and materials were superlative. Jay and Barbara loved the notion that their house felt like an English Georgian manor, and even considering all their fine American antiques, they wanted to reinforce that connection.

Along with structural changes—expanded closets, a new kitchen with an added mudroom and servants' bathroom—we made a number of subtle architectural

Opposite:
The eighteenth-century marble mantel in the living room holds Chinese Export porcelain. Hanging on the wall is a Regency needlepoint bellpull—nowadays used purely as decoration!

Red-lined shelves holding some of the Reibels' collection of Lowestoft china flank the archway to the entry hall.

Opposite:
The Fuchsia Arch wallpaper in the entrance hall is outlined with a red wallpaper fillet. On the wood floor is a French Empire needlepoint rug.

adjustments. I am a big believer in arches: they give oomph—a sense of parade or ceremony—especially between major rooms. We installed a large classical arch between the vast entry hall and the living room, making the joint space an excellent and fluid area for entertaining.

In the entry hall and staircase, we left in place the previous owner's wallpaper—the trellis-arched Victorian Fuchsia Arch design used in Leixlip Castle—but ratcheted up the intensity by outlining the room with a darkish red wallpaper fillet. This caused some consternation. "We thought the idea was *awful*,"

The living room incorporates a mix of furniture and patterns. Curtains are of Pillement, a chinoiserie toile.

says Jay, "but Keith stood his ground. He said, 'Wait until you see everything in its place.' He was right, of course. It worked brilliantly." Old Oriental rugs and a beautiful floral French Empire needlepoint rug lay on the polished wood floor. Furnishings included a refined antique Hepplewhite curved settee with a Regency-inspired, thin-striped, red and white cover. On the walls were old prints and reverse-glass paintings of ships.

In the living room, we glazed the paneled walls in three tones of creamy bone to match the background of the lively red and cream Pillement chinoiserie toile curtains. The mantel was a simple, classical, eighteenth-century marble one

The finely detailed, dark green faux paneling in the library is lightened by the anaglypta ceiling, Garbo carpeting, and Tree Peony linen.

with fine Chinese Export porcelain (collected by the Reibels) on the shelf. An arrangement of American silhouettes surrounded an elegant circular gesso and parcel-gilt English rococo mirror that appeared to hang from a pert green ribbon sash and bow. An enticing mix of furniture and seating groups was united by two beautiful antique rugs, one an Indian Agra, the other a bold, floral English Regency needlepoint. This alluring room grabbed visitors and drew them right in.

Also off the entry hall was the paneled library. When the Reibels found the house, the room had been planked in crude knotty pine—"naughty pine," as my long-time client Drue Heinz would say. We created faux paneling with molding

A bay in the dining room holds a small table. Red Regency-style swags provide a theatrical touch.

on sheetrock. The mock panels were painted, stipple-glazed in forest green, and then wiped to bring out the paler color of the last under-coat. We carpeted the poor-quality wood floor in one of our favorite broadloom patterns—the Bessarabian-style Garbo. Festoon blinds and most of the upholstery for the comfortable furniture were in Colefax & Fowler's Tree Peony linen (different from Lee Jofa's design of similar name). The ceiling was plaster-patterned in anaglypta. The brass wall sconces and chandelier were silver-plated—a finish that really does something magical against strong dark walls. Though the library is less than half the size of the living room, people love to crowd into the cozy, inviting space.

Leading off the other side of the entry hall was the formal dining room with a large bay window. This bay held a delicate-looking oval breakfast table and some of a set of stylish painted English elbow chairs—other members of the set wander throughout the house. A chimney breast was covered in mirrored glass; etched-green-glass sconces were set atop the mirrored surface. The rest of the room was wrapped in a rare and exciting eighteenth-century hand-painted Chinese scenic paper from the Qianlong period, which we discovered at Gracie & Sons. "When Keith took me to Gracie, we went with the intention of finding a reproduction paper," said Jay. "After about half an hour, Mr. Gracie realized that I was really interested, and he showed us this 1760 Chinese hand-painted paper. It was very costly, of course, but the other papers couldn't compare." The paper was restored to perfection by Gracie's charming Mr. Woo and then installed in the dining

The dining room table is surrounded by mahogany splat-back chairs alternating with Chinese Chippendale mahogany armchairs. The predominant feature is the antique Chinese scenic wallpaper.

room; an evening there was like dining in a fantastic landscape peopled with large figures in the foreground and tiny figures in the distance. With this kind of old paper—and it is a blessing!—there is no need to buy any paintings, which would only compete. In fact, real eighteenth-century hand-painted wallpaper panels are themselves meaningful pieces of fine art: they cost as much and, like a painting or sculpture, can move from house to house, as long as they have been properly mounted over muslin. In all my years of dealing with

A passage lined in Brunschwig's Treillage wallpaper is visually expanded by the mirrored panels of the French doors.

Opposite:
A peacock-colored arched ceiling and droll upside-down umbrella chandelier dramatize the sunroom.

antique wallpaper panels, the only Qianlong I ever saw that could hold a candle to the Reibels' was the equally well-peopled antique paper showing a Chinese wedding procession in Rudolf Nureyev's scintillating dining room in his apartment in the Dakota in Manhattan.

A corridor off the large main hall led to coat closets and a powder room. We installed more arches as well as French doors with mirrored panels and a bold black and white marble floor. The walls and ceiling were papered in green and white Treillage paper; the attendant wallpaper friezes, cornices, and pilasters were used to great architectural effect.

Between the dining room and the kitchen was a passage to an amusing sunroom. It had unusual arched windows and an extraordinary groin-vaulted ceiling, which we stipple-glazed in peacock green. Painted rattan furniture and bright sunshiny fabrics induced smiles in this comfortable hideaway.

I told the Reibels not to visit while we were installing the house. "We're fussy," said Jay, "and we like to attend to details, but we stayed away for almost three weeks! Then when we saw it, with music playing and champagne to sip, we just fell in love with it." Their daughter Kate, who was eight when they moved, commented recently, "You know, Keith did an amazing job. Nothing has changed." And Jay Reibel, fifteen years down the road, says the house is "still great, but aging quietly . . . like all of us."

"Vexy Rexy"

ONE OF MY old stalwarts, Drue Heinz, of the 57 Varieties family, first recommended me to the Rex Harrisons. The Harrisons' first utterance—"We are not in the same league as Mrs. Heinz. We have only *one* variety"—was eerily similar to that of my old-time client Joseph Mankiewicz (another Heinz connection).

The Harrisons' first appearance in Irvine & Fleming's office was nothing if not theatrical. Rex's sixth wife, Mercia (an Anglo-Indian beauty—but then, all of them were gorgeous), always nonpareil elegant, delivered her next good line as she slid out of a cobalt-dyed Dior fur shrug: "We are going to have to be very thrifty. We don't get a million dollars a movie anymore." Sexy Rexy, silent at first and fussing with his Captain Shotover beard (he was appearing on Broadway in the acclaimed production of *Heartbreak House*), suddenly said, "I think he's a complete phony. He doesn't sound *remotely* Scottish." Apparently Drue Heinz had told him that since I was Scottish, he would find me very simpatico. I think he was expecting me to sound like a poor man's Sean Connery!

Rex and Mercia had bought a Manhattan aerie high over the East River in one of the most romantic apartment houses in Manhattan. Over the years, it was home to many luminaries: Lord Rothermere, Greta Garbo (who was allowed to ride the elevator in solitary splendor—as I saw with my own eyes), Drue Heinz, Valentina, Alexander Woollcott, Mrs. John Barry Ryan (Otto Kahn's daughter), and on and on. Rex, as though addressing a roomful of Eliza Doolittles, said of the flat, "What I like is old-fashioned Englishness. My spouse, alas, has a contemporary yearning." But I amused—and reassured—him by noting that our firm is known for a sense of humor when it comes to combining the tastes of couples with different outlooks.

Opposite:
Against one wall in the living room is a long, black-lacquered Chinese altar table flanked by two Giacometti armchairs.

The original long entrance hall of the apartment was transformed into a library/dining room. The English Regency chairs with Pompeian decorations were bought in London in a dilapidated state and restored by Chippy.

Though endlessly fascinating, Rex Harrison had a short fuse. Doors slammed and sudden storms blew up throughout the job. Once, just after he had erupted and stomped into his bathroom, I glimpsed his crest-embroidered silk-velvet slippers on the floor of his dressing room. I threw them after him and shouted, "Damn, damn, damn!" What a nasty glare I got, followed slowly by an oh-so-painful smile.

As the job took off, my assistant, Sam Blount, and I focused on space planning and construction. The dining room of the previous owners, with its good north light, was sacrificed to make a painting studio for Rex, who was beginning to work in oils. Mercia, always practical, decreed, "Oils and turpentine *stink* so. You want to be at the far end of the apartment, Harry!" (She always called him Harry.)

Mercia was full of other well-digested ideas. She, Sam, and I figured out that we could move the closets out of the front hall and then rework the space as a glittering gem of a library/dining room/hall. There was room enough for a table for eight; another table could be set up in the adjoining drawing room ("I don't know what a *living room* really is!" complained Harrison-as-Higgins) for a larger dinner. The hall became one of the most spectacular spaces I have ever decorated. Its walls and bookcases—stacked with Oscar and Tony awards—were stipple-glazed in dark ink blue, spattered with paler blue and black, and highlighted with faux-tortoise pilasters. The shelves were edged with black-leather gilt-embossed strips. This is an old tradition in libraries: in the eighteenth century—and before—cut or pinked felt or baize strips were applied to the front edges of bookshelves so that the top of each book was gently dusted as it was withdrawn.

At the back of this hall was a banquette—Rex's throne at dinner parties. Over it hung a portrait of some stately lady by Sir Joshua Reynolds. I had really

A scarlet wallpaper fillet delineates the blue and yellow color scheme in the living room.

wanted to hang the likeness over the mantel in the drawing room, but Rex, raising his eyebrows to express the highest degree of incredulity, said, "Certainly not! Only one's true ancestors may hang over a mantelpiece." No ancestors were at hand, though, so over the mantel in the bright and sunny drawing room we hung a beautiful Pissarro flanked by a Milton Avery and a Dunoyer de Segonzac, a combination that suited the spirit of the room far better.

The drawing room was lined in a spanking bright yellow striped wallpaper spiced with a thin red paper fillet outline. The overstuffed furniture was upholstered in an English bird and floral chinoiserie chintz with a bold yellow background; the design glowed in front of the pine recessed bookcases and mantel. Mercia's iron Giacometti chairs and black-lacquer Chinese altar table were complemented by a mix of traditional wood pieces and black-lacquer Regency chairs. The floor was covered in an unexpected Wilton-weave wool Antelope carpet— a touch of saucy theatrical whimsy. Heavy festoon blinds were made of sky blue and white pinstriped satin. Why would anyone want curtains that would have shut out all the light? Rex Harrison once said, "New York and Venice both jump up out of the water in the most brazen defiance of gravity. The movement of light is similar in these two old port cities."

In my comings and goings to the apartment once the Harrisons were established, it always warmed the cockles of my northern Scottish heart to see that almost all of the windows were partly open, drawing delectable cool zephyrs from the Statue of Liberty. Indeed, every room in the apartment—even the bathroom—looked out over water and that intense American light. During the course of the job, the queen knighted Rex Harrison, and after our work wrapped up, we shared some very jolly times with Sir Rex and Lady Harrison—trips to London, lunches at the Ritz, visits backstage. Chippy and I were invited to star-studded dinners at the apartment; one time, I sat next to the legendary Claudette Colbert. Mercia took a serious interest in fine cooking, but that never stopped her from being the ideal front-and-center hostess. What a happy time it was! Possibly what tickled me most was that Rex (a bit like me, perhaps) was quick and naughty and had a schoolboy's impish charm. 🐾

Opposite:
Over the antique carved-pine mantel hangs a painting by Pissarro. The two bronze lion sculptures are by Giacometti, a friend of Mercia's.

Consummate New Yorkers

I T WAS ABOUT 1983 when Steven and Cynthia Brill first approached us. The two had met at Yale Law School. ("Well, technically," says Cynthia, "in the law school building. I studied law at NYU and we met at Yale through a friend.") Steven was soon off on his meteoric media rise: writing serious books (*The Teamsters* was a triumph); founding the enormously successful magazine *American Lawyer;* producing articles for *New York* magazine and a column for *Esquire;* and founding the electrifying (if controversial) cable station Court TV and the media magazine *Brill's Content*. His massively researched *After* detailed post-9/11 events. Cynthia was his constant confidant, top lieutenant, and legal advisor. Although they were star performers among the hard-working professionals of New York City, family always came first, I observed. Even ultra-busy Steven spent serious quality time with their three kids.

The couple's Fifth Avenue apartment had breathtaking views across Central Park and down the avenue. Cynthia remembers, "I had seen some interiors in the *New York Times Magazine* that I really liked. Though I had never heard of Irvine & Fleming before, I called them up. I was asked to go to their office—more, I think, for them to interview *me* than the other way around." Our work was ongoing, with regular adjustments for the Brills' growing family. Over time, the library was corralled to become a room for their younger daughter, and the dining room was siphoned off to make a bedroom for their son.

The Brills coped for a time. They could always escape to their estate in upper Westchester, which I also helped to decorate. By the beginning of the new century, however, they were putting serious time into trying to find a bigger Manhattan apartment. But Cynthia could not find one that suited. So she asked me to take a walk through the old apartment in the hope that I could imagine a

Opposite:
A Regency bull's-eye mirror of carved laurel leaves reflects the living room.

solution for their overcrowded life. I took my assistant, Jason Bell, who had a flair for space planning, and we came up with a fairly radical way to create a library and dining room and also to reconfigure the rooms of the two daughters, who would soon be heading off to college.

We decided to revamp the old entry hall, a long but wasted space that had devolved into a dumping ground, with an enfilade of architectural arches that would create a series of rooms. Hidden pocket doors could isolate each space as necessary. We would have a small entrance hall, a large library, a tiny, charming dining room, and just past a screen of columns and pilasters, the living room.

Once we had made these plans, *speed* became the priority. The Brills could spend the summer camping out, but they had to be reinstalled in their New York pad by Labor Day. Impossible! But our contractors, Jane and Alex Marinas of A & J Alterations, were not only amusing but efficient, and magically we made it—*just!* It was certainly the fastest construction job Irvine & Fleming had ever pulled off.

We took the decoration of the new spaces in a fresh direction. "Keith told us it was time we had a grown-up apartment," said Cynthia. The architectural bookcases, overscaled molding, recessed plasma television, and stereo in the library hall were faux-painted as bleached pine. The interiors of the bookcases were deep red, and the groin-vaulted ceiling was stippled in azure. The comfy furniture was covered in a delightful English hand-blocked print of fire birds and foliage from Robert Kime.

The tiny dining room, beyond the next arch, had a coffered ceiling constructed in steps; my favorite version of a Gucci stripe added drama to the space. Serving units and china cupboards were concealed in the walls. Above the white-glazed, paneled dado, we hung an exemplary Chinese scenic paper depicting a

White American Directoire chairs and Chinese scenic wallpaper create a garden setting in the Brills' city dining room.

Opposite:
In the library hall, red glazing on the bookcase interiors throws them forward. The recess is mirrored, so the bookcases look as if they go on forever.

An early-nineteenth-century lacquered bureau in the living room is centered between built-in bookcases. The mirror behind reflects the room.

Opposite:
A corner of the living room with curtains in the linen print Tree Peony.

garden full of exotic plants and birds. A paper like this pushes out the walls of a room; here, diners were transported into a picturesque grove. A gleaming acajou French Empire expandable dining table was surrounded by leather-covered, painted Directoire chairs. The rug was one of our favorites, the red and brown Rocksavage.

A glazed and faux-stone-finished screen of columns and pilasters led from the dining room to the living room, where walls were glazed in a pale creamy strié. The upholstery and curtain fabric we used was a bold English print on linen called Tree Peony; its turquoise-green amid a sea of cream and beige was strongly compatible with the faded Sultanabad rug. On the east wall, a mirrored panel between painted bookcases reflected the spectacular view through the windows on the opposite wall; the mirror also brought in light, giving the effect of a much larger room.

"The apartment was perfect for our needs," said Cynthia, "but if someone had shown me the combination of wallpaper, rug, and ceiling, I would have thought them crazy. In the end, they work so well together. You just have to throw your trust to Keith." I hope the Brills will be happily ensconced in their New York apartment for at least the next twenty years, and so I said to Cynthia, "Next time, don't call me. I'll be pushing up daisies!"

Tidewater Virginia in the Midwest

OVER THE YEARS, we have worked on many golf and country clubs, but never one so vast or important as the New Albany Country Club in the purlieus of Columbus, Ohio. Business genius Leslie Wexner was the magician pulling the strings behind the project. He selected as architect the renowned Jaquelin Robertson, leader of the prolific and talented firm Cooper, Robertson & Partners. Robertson is a southern gentleman, an architect of the Tidewater Georgian style. He had grown up in a house designed by William Lawrence Bottomley, a great early-twentieth-century Georgian revivalist. Irvine & Fleming was chosen from a bevy of serious competitors. Our nice Ohio clients Jack and Charlotte Kessler and Roger Sahli, Wexner's personal architect and Tom Fleming's longtime friend, helped along the decision. Networking certainly does oil the wheels of our little world!

Les Wexner was almost inhumanly distant, surrounded by a moat of power and its trappings—yachts, private jets, and super-grand houses—and separated from us by hordes of yes-men. We had many intense group meetings where Wexner's second team interrupted and criticized as I attempted to explain developing ideas. Finally, I asked Mr. Wexner if he wanted to listen to us professionals, or just to his support team. The conference room cleared instantly, leaving him, Tom, and me. Mr. Wexner icily queried every decision and every detail (this kind of concentrated involvement was why his businesses—Limited Stores, Express, Victoria's Secret, and more—were such astounding successes), and in the next hour, we had 80 percent of the design worked out and an approximate budget approved. Wexner kept on top of every nuance that intrigued him. During one of our conferences, he asked if either of us had been to Mark's Club in London— one of the stylish private dining clubs conceived and owned by Sir Mark Birley.

Opposite:
Passages leading to restaurants and locker rooms are elegantly curved and sprinkled with busts on plinths, hall tables, and side chairs.

263

A Savonnerie carpet cut down from one in Mrs. Cornelius Vanderbilt's New York apartment dominates the entrance hall.

When I answered no, Les Wexner insisted that both Tom and I must take the Concorde that weekend to have a look. The next moment, a wry smile crossed his visage, and he added, "Well, *one* of you can go on the Concorde!"

The inspiration for the country club—architecture and decoration—came from the great Georgian Colonial plantation houses of Virginia: Stratford Hall (the greatest) on the Potomac, Carter's Grove on the James, Kenmore on the Rappahannock, and so many more. The quality of antiques we used was superlative. We shopped all over England. The final results were extraordinarily personal and gave each room real depth and character. As we walked away from the splashy opening party, Jaque Robertson, always scrupulously polite, said, "Keith, not one of them realizes that in ten years this whole place will look ten times better than it does now."

Wide Georgian steps led to a massive front door and then to a riveting entry hall with a coved ceiling above a substantial cornice. The walls were papered in our favorite Pembroke Damask outlined with a sharp red paper fillet. Two facing carved, bleached-pine eagle consoles with green marble tops (they must have been gilded in the eighteenth century and later stripped) punctuate the two long

The drawing room walls are paneled and inset with nineteenth-century Zuber scenic wallpaper. Textured cotton damask upholstery is embellished with a custom-worked outline of deep red chain stitch.

Columns and screens divide the music room from the drawing room. On the walls is one of a pair of Louis XVI mirrors.

walls. On the floor was an eighteenth-century Savonnerie rug, its colors vibrant against a dark brown background—it is the ultimate welcome mat! Its provenance was unusual: it was in fact a remnant, cut down and re-formed, from an enormous rug used in Mrs. Cornelius Vanderbilt's salon on Fifth Avenue in New York. I own an early-twentieth-century Walter Thompson painting of this room, and the design is clearly recognizable.

Past the entrance hall was the club drawing room. The wall-to-wall carpet was a geometric design copied by Colefax & Fowler from a Regency rug. It was specially custom-woven to withstand golfers' spikes. We installed two fireplaces

266

on the long sides of the room, each dressed with a graceful eighteenth-century Scottish carved-pine mantel. Nineteenth-century Zuber wallpaper panels of hunting scenes were inset on the softly glazed walls. We thus avoided having to buy art for the walls—but the panels *were* art, giving the room a feeling of expanded space plus a sense of history. Intimate seating groups were scattered about; since members used the drawing room as a passageway, we anchored the middle with a round English Regency pedestal table holding an oversized black and gold chinoiserie pot. A nineteenth-century crystal chandelier shimmered overhead.

Behind two handsome black-lacquer screens at the far end of the room was the music room, complete with grand piano as well as space enough for a small group of musicians. Black-leather-covered furniture showed up well against walls paneled and glazed in pearl tones. Two Louis XVI carved and painted mirrors, both surrounded by groups of antique engravings of classical figures topped with carved oval medallions, reflected each other across the music room, and two classical busts sat on faux-marbled plinths. I am always pushing busts. One of my most charming clients, the late Ken Auchincloss, was someone I nagged endlessly about this; the last time I saw him across noisy Madison Avenue, he yelled to me, "Keith! You can *never* have too many busts, or too many columns!"

The corridors on either side of the central block are gently curved, similar to the corridors at Kedleston Hall in Derbyshire. Patterned red carpeting leads to restaurants and other subsidiary areas, and the passages are punctuated by side tables, chairs—and more busts.

The Buxton carpeting on the main staircase was based on an antique design.

The upper walls of the main staircase were hung with sporting prints and paintings; interspersed was a collection of antique trophy deer antlers. A vast carved and gilded triple chandelier floats above a vivid Buxton carpet by Colefax & Fowler. The Axminster Buxton was based on one that belonged to John Vere Brown, my dear friend since college days at Kingston Art School. Imogen Taylor had asked him if Colefax & Fowler could copy the pattern, and being no businessman, he readily agreed. When the new carpeting started rolling off the loom at Avena, the mill in Yorkshire—made from all that good wool from the Dales— the firm gave John a measly hall rug, a sop considering that Colefax & Fowler, and all its international outlets, sold miles of Buxton all over the world. We at Irvine & Fleming have used a wealth of it ourselves.

The sports bar near the men's locker room complex was a rustic half-brother to New York's well-seasoned 21 Club—and it was great fun to pull off. Rough plastered walls were antiqued by waxing and hand-polishing. The darker-glazed ceiling was hung with model planes, satellites, and cars, and the walls were peppered with an idiosyncratic collection of pictures—oil paintings, prints, license plates, historic golf and political photographs, and even some 1940s Vargas girls. The tavern tables were surrounded by oak Windsor chairs, all sitting on a bright MacKenzie wool tartan carpet. It was beer-and-pretzel heaven— another theater set by Irvine & Fleming—but one that has proved to have easy-to-live-with permanence.

The New Albany Club was, for us, a big job. As a rule, Tom Fleming and I meet clients together and then work on separate jobs, but this one was a successful team effort. Tom says, "Maybe our relationship over the years hasn't all been a bowl of cherries, but we sure have tried to make it that. Keith has perhaps the best sense of humor of anyone I know—and mine isn't too bad, either! I think we both credit that for getting us through over forty-five years. Of course he has talent—more in one little finger than most of us in our whole body. That I certainly respect—after all, he taught me all I know. After decorating, and that sense of humor, I think Keith's best talent is teaching. Since 1959, he has taught many neophytes—like me. I had no formal training in the field. Maybe someday he'll do it on a more formal basis."

Opposite:
A nod to New York's 21 Club, the sports bar is adorned with objects—mostly vintage forms of transport—hung from the ceiling and memorabilia on the walls. Tavern tables and oak Windsor chairs provide a casual atmosphere.

Old Society Magic

M RS. HOWARD ROSS—Nanette—is a scintillating California-born blond with the heart and style of a true New Yorker. She has the figure of a wood nymph and wears clothes like a dream, and her annual calendar moves her through Palm Beach, Manhattan, and Newport. Nanette came to us first through a son and daughter-in-law, Jim and Alice Ross, and then through a daughter and son-in-law, Debbie (my star!) and Philippe Dauman. My first project with Nanette was a spacious apartment in the Everglades Club in Palm Beach, one of Addison Mizner's enduring successes. The apartment had vast rooms with lovely 1920s tile floors and old cypress beams and doors. By the time our work was done, we had a toe in the door of Mrs. Ross's enormous apartment in New York.

Nanette, herself a dilettante decorator, had sure tastes but was reaching higher and deeper. The moment we stepped into Colefax & Fowler's London shop (run by the nice Roger Jones), she caught onto the look of played-down grandeur and set her sights on a much more European target. Mrs. Ross's Park Avenue apartment was in one of New York's top prewar buildings. Over the years, I have become well aware that a dozen or so exemplary apartment blocks rise in stature above so many others. Many of the "swells" with whom we have crossed paths have at one time or another hung their hats in one of these great buildings. Nanette Ross's apartment house, completed in 1929, was designed by Rosario Candela—responsible for many of New York's most luxurious apartment buildings—and Cross & Cross. Her apartment had been part of a triplex—with its own ballroom, mind you—and was once, I have been told, the biggest apartment in Manhattan.

The impressive entrance hall was long and gallerylike with a curiously low ceiling with recessed lights. Upon investigating, we discovered Aladdin's cave

The monumental Gothic stone window in the library draped in La Portugaise linen.

Opposite:
In the Renaissance-style entry gallery, walls glazed in pale shrimp stand out beautifully against the wood doors with stone trim.

I took a quick rest as Mrs. Ross's apartment neared completion.

The drawing room, paneled in eighteenth-century mahogany, features an eclectic mix of French floral chintzes all sitting on a Savonnerie rug.

above. An extraordinary vaulted ceiling soared another five feet; handsome carved-oak beams with bosses, each with a different face hand-modeled at the end, complemented the hall's carved-oak doors. But Aladdin's cave was also a craftsman's disaster. Whoever installed the dropped ceiling had knocked off chunks of wood and drilled rough holes in the old beams. Months of complicated restoration would extend the whole job.

Yet there was a silver lining. Our inquisitive minds piqued, we decided to take a closer look at the library. And we found another treasure: it was actually a double-height space, with a ceiling even more elaborate than that of the gallery. Not only that, but the existing window was revealed to be an overscaled, lead-paned, Gothic oriel aperture with stone mullions—big bucks even in the 1920s!

While we were restoring these magnificent discoveries and incorporating them into the design—and there was no question that we would do this—we tackled the space planning for the rest of the apartment. We created a procession of unusual and architecturally imaginative dressing rooms that spun out from an octagonal center all of mirrored and beveled French doors. Atop the octagon was an antique cupola dome with a painted Florentine umbrella chandelier. How sparkling it was—but almost impossible to photograph!

The gloriously refurbished entry gallery was rough-glazed in a glowing shrimp color that played off well against the faded oak beams and doors. We papered the ceiling peaks in overlapping squares of silver and gold metallic paper, and on the floor was our favorite Rocksavage rug in brown and dark coral. We slipcovered a number of Queen Anne chairs—part of a set of about twenty-four that floated from place to place—in off-white linen; their red piping

The burgundy-lacquered bar is inlaid with brass strips and highlights. The English oak linen-fold paneled door was original to the apartment.

Opposite:
Raspberry stippled walls bring drama to the library. Through the stone arch is the door to the bar.

and monogramming was an idea I had seen at the Duke of Beaufort's Badminton House, decorated by Tom Parr of Colefax & Fowler. An arresting Charles II red-lacquer chinoiserie cabinet on a rococo carved base groaned under a collection of blue and white Chinese pots, and in the center of the gallery was a round table skirted in a rich coral and gold Fortuny damask design. A pair of sparkling Regency-style chandelier lanterns delineated the length of the space.

The dining room had been paneled in the 1920s and was boldly simple but full of well-carved details. These paneled walls were glazed and highlighted in a *ton-sur-ton* palette of yellowing bone to imitate a Georgian room, a nice accompaniment for the real Georgian English carved mantel. Instead of a formal expandable table and a sea of chairs, Mrs. Ross preferred two round skirted tables that could each seat six to eight guests. This relaxed arrangement was more conducive to lively conversation. An orange cotton French print was used for the table skirts, and the remaining Queen Anne chairs were covered in a rather saucy miniature faux-animal print. Silk curtains were made in a multicolored Italian woven stripe. Two early Tang horses, which we found at an Olympia antiques fair in London, stood sentinel on an elegant Regency serving table.

The most atmospheric room in an apartment brimming with atmosphere was the library. It was super-comfortable and all-enveloping—like a much-loved cashmere overcoat. The walls were stippled in dark raspberry lacquer, a color that glowed against the cold stone mullions of the vast Gothic window. A glimpse past the lacquered walls and through the windows' leaded panes at the brash yellow New York taxicabs scurrying along Park Avenue was an almost surreal juxtaposition. The Bessarabian Garbo carpeting provided a foil for an assortment of strong English antiques. The sofa and Regency-style swags and jabots at the window were made of La Portugaise linen. A charming Georgian oil of a small girl

The focal point of the dining room is an extraordinary eighteenth-century English carved-marble mantel. The room is always set up with two round tables surrounded by leopard-print-covered chairs.

Opposite:
Holding the center of the entry gallery is a Fortuny damask–draped table. A Charles II red-lacquer cabinet holds pieces from Mrs. Ross's vast collection of blue and white porcelain.

Eighteenth-century steel engravings in round and oval frames around an unusual black and gilt Regency mirror in the bedroom seating area.

was surrounded by a set of tinted steel engravings, depicting the popular French romance *Paul et Virginie*, in their original modish frames.

Nanette's bedroom was a romantic fantasy, a blithe and flattering sea of pink pinstripes on the walls and cushions, green and pink highlighting and glazing on the trim, a green and white carpet of leaf trellises, and miles and miles of the Rope Lattice chintz so beloved by John Fowler. Some of the pillows had designs of Staffordshire figures. The room was enriched by a mixture of mirrors, prints,

At the foot of the draped and painted canopy bed is a black and gold Regency window seat.

silhouettes, and watercolors, including two beautiful drypoint etchings by Paul Helleu. On the green baize padded door—which apes those that separate the fancy folk from the servants in the great houses of England—was Nanette Ross's monogram picked out in French nails. It harked back to one I made for Vivien Leigh in London; she particularly loved its slightly theatrical feel. I have used the idea many times for clients, not always in green. Mrs. Ross blooms with radiance in her splendid Manhattan gem.

A Summer Place

I FIRST MET Diane and John Samuels in the 1980s. They had led a Washington, D.C., life before moving to Greenwich, Connecticut. John, a high-powered corporate lawyer, had been in government administration and is now in the hierarchy of a major American company. The attractive couple have two equally dazzling daughters, Emily and Sarah. We pulled together the Samuels' charming house in Greenwich with the furniture, and even some of the curtains, from their Washington home. We were able to give it drama, but it was still inviting.

Every summer, the Samuels spent a family holiday on Nantucket, usually in a rented house. But at the end of the 1990s, John and Diane found a perfect lot in a perfect location on the island and decided to build. They worked on plans with the Pennsylvania architect Lyman Perry, who had done a lot of work on Nantucket. We were part of the project team from day one. John recently told Chippy, "When we spoke to the architects, we said we wanted something that looked as if it was grandmother's—as if it had some history. They understood, and so did Keith." A traditional, weathered-shingle East Coast cottage expressed the Samuels' ideas perfectly (and also complied with the stringent architectural rules governing new construction on the island).

Architectural details on the interior were also inspired by the New England coastal tradition. Wainscoting flows through the house, mostly at that "bosom" height so beloved at the turn-of-the-century before last. Also called Philadelphia grooved siding or tongue and groove, the wainscoting, painted a light and cheerful creamy white, started at the front door and continued

An overscaled bull's-eye mirror reflects a carved American eagle atop an English Regency pine console table.

Opposite:
On the front hall table is a late-eighteenth-century sailor's hat. Such hats were waterproofed with tar—hence the use of "tars" for sailors. Above, is a Regency bull's-eye mirror, unusual because it has a bleached pine frame. The rug is antique Samarkand, and the chair is country Chippendale.

Three Guatemalan area rugs in different weaves delineate the family room. The sofa is upholstered in Le Zebre, a cotton and linen print from Brunschwig, and the large check is Plaid from Henry Calvin Fabrics.

through widening halls to a more expansive space at the bottom of the stair-case. Opposite the stairs stood an impressive antique English pine console table topped with an assortment of nautical Liverpool Transfer pottery and a carved American eagle, which John and Diane had bought in New Hampshire. Above the wainscoting, a subtle beige and white damask design wallpaper with easy American hand-blocked looks swept up three floors of the center of the house, providing a perfect backdrop for a growing collection of drawings and wash drawings of old ships.

The staircase hall led to the large family room, the true center of the house. In our close-to-servantless society, these rooms have become the only way to maintain a comfortable continuity of family life. Living rooms and libraries, on the other hand, have become unused showplaces reserved mainly for guests, just as they were more than a century ago.

The Samuels' family room was simple and comfortable, its cool, clean lines anchored with rustic pieces and simple but attractive antiques. The overall palette was soft natural and beige, sparked into life by lively French blue touches—especially in the stylized 1950s Dahlia print used on the comfy overstuffed chair and ottoman (shades of Veronica Lake and Alan Ladd in *The Blue Dahlia*). The color reminded me of the blue of French porters' uniforms in Paris years ago, or of the blue of sugar packets from my childhood. Throw rugs in differing, natural modern weaves were made in Guatemala. At the far end of the room was an enormous window seat, slathered with assorted pillows and fronted by two odd nineteenth-century Chinese teak opium tables. Flanking the fireplace with its antique Massachusetts mantel were a rush-seated Scottish Orkney chair and a rustic English Regency painted elbow chair—two nations united but one soul divided!

Among the unusual architectural features in the house were two tiny, rather romantic, book-lined passages on either side of the fireplace; these led to a small living room. This room, a smidge more sophisticated, was almost a return to the nineteenth-century parlor. The trim and cabinetwork were highlight-glazed. A faded-to-obscurity Oushak rug rested on the floor. The predominantly beige

The oversized window seat is smothered in a mix of pillows.

The eighteenth-century portrait of an American sea captain in the living room was painted in China for the export trade. The curtains are in Brunschwig's Paros stripe; the sofa is covered in Cowtan & Tout's Eton check.

palette was jumped up by a shocking and attractive red, pink, and oyster check on the sofa, and a pink and red chinoiserie toile on cushions and some of the chairs. The bookcases were crammed with Diane's collection of blue and white Canton china. The portrait to the right of one window became the lodestar and "genius of the place."

The library across the hall was more traditional altogether, a concession to John, the family conservative. (Diane is more cutting-edge and pared down—in both her dress and her tastes.) The walls were painted and glazed in wrapping-paper brown with a strié mini-stripe, a warm background for the traditional English chintz—its blue ticking background a foil for its floral exuberance—used

In the master bedroom, cream-painted cupboards and drawers are built into the walls. The contemporary American four-poster bed and the blanket chest at its foot are both milk-painted blue.

for the curtains and some of the furniture. The interiors of the bookcases were painted cranberry red. The largest sofa, a blast from the 1940s, was dark, *dark* green—a staple of my early days in decorating. Everything old is new again.

The floor had a couple of nice old "dying" Oriental rugs—practical because they never show signs of wear. There were some odd, not too grand pieces of Georgian wood furniture, an old Adirondack wood rocker, a model of a Swedish fishing boat, and two reproduction Canton pots made into lamps and given astonishing shades of Delft blue pleated cotton. Scenic walls—views of Nantucket harbor painted and antiqued on canvas by the artists at Gracie & Sons in Manhattan—bestowed great character on the tiny wainscoted powder room.

Upstairs, the master bedroom suite was a haven of peace and repose, early American spare but cozy and modern at the same time. It was composed around Colefax & Fowler's tried-and-true Plumbago cotton print (in real life, this is quite one of my most *un*-favorite flowers) with its unusual purplish-lavender tones of blue. There was a simple blue-painted American post bed, an enormous ship of a high-backed lounging sofa covered in beige and white mattress ticking, a modern painted Scandinavian open armchair, and a modern natural and blue check cotton rug. To one side was a Plumbago-covered window seat to curl up on and survey the ocean. Altogether, the bedroom was a summer dream.

When I suggested a green toile bedroom for Emily—"all toile, everywhere!"—John Samuels became alarmed. "Trust me," I replied. "He'd said that before, and we had trusted him, but this time I was really dubious," said John. "Now it's my favorite bedroom." He also loves his third- floor office and study. Three floors are unusual on Nantucket, but the architects used a gambrel roof, which is higher in the center, to abide by the island's height restrictions.

Around the house were three porches that functioned almost like outside rooms. They overlooked a spectacular garden. "It feels as if we have put down roots," said Diane. The house and garden, almost miraculously, look as if they have been in existence for a long time, and certainly they will last for future generations.

When all was complete, Diane wrote to me, "Keith, John and I just love this house. You really listened to what we wanted to create and captured that feeling beyond our wildest dreams. In the years I've known you, you've taught me a lot—I've learned to appreciate color, recognize affordable antiques, and everywhere spot and smile at all the special Keith touches. Mostly though, I've learned to trust you as a designer, and as a friend, and to endlessly enjoy the beautiful rooms you create." 🐾

On the porch, cushions and back-rests of bottle green and white stripes from Sunbrella complement the dark wicker furniture.

Opposite:
A welcoming sofa and chaise in a serene nook.

Photography Credits

The authors and the publisher have made every effort to identify owners of copyrighted material. Any omissions will be rectified in future editions. Numbers refer to page numbers.

Michel Arnaud: 118, 130, 132–35, 137
Eric Boman: 58–63, 144, 146–51
Richard Champion: 152–55
Billy Cunningham: 30–35, 142, 144–47, 198, 199, 262, 264–68
Tom Fleming: 64–67, 100, 101
Oberto Gili: 96, 98, 99, 280–87
John Hall: 120, 123
Lizzie Himmel: Frontispiece, 70, 71, 95, 186, 188–93, 200–2, 204–7
Horst: 6, 156–61
Reprinted by permission from *House Beautiful,* copyright 2005. Hearst Communications, Inc. All rights reserved. Thibault Jeanson, photographer: 270–79
Thibault Jeanson: 176–185
Alex McLean: 74, 117, 119, 121, 122, 124–28, 131, 214, 216, 218, 219
Derry Moore: 76, 78–81, 83
Michael Mundy: 220–27
Karen Radkai: 68, 69, 72, 73, 234, 236, 237, 239
Simon Upton: 84–91, 162, 164–68, 170–75
John Vere Brown: 92, 94, 97, 102–4, 105 (top), 106, 107, 109–16
Peter Vitale: 41–45, 240, 242–49, 250, 252, 253, 255
Jonathan Wallen: 10
Susan Wood: 22, 24–29, 46, 47, 49–57

Bob and Pat Schiffer. Lady Christabel Aberconway.
Mrs. Oakleigh Thorne. Fifi Fell. Gunie and Mohan
Murjani. Lady Henrietta and Mr. Edward St. George.
Tom and Joseph Gal. Penny and Clarence Dauphinot.
Alexandra Whitney. ~~Emilie and John Dickie.~~
Theresa Coolidge. Carol and Michael Smith.
Anne Fuchs Sutherland. Peggy and Martin Byman.
Mone Altenor Patino. Ambassador Robert Stuart.
Marnie and Donaldson Pillsbury. Joan Crawford.
~~Christopher Hussee.~~ Molly, Duchess of Buccleugh.
Frances and Richard Borty. Peggy and Jean de
Bertholet. Pam and Herman Whiton. Diana Ross.
Barbara Isles. Jeffrey Berenson. Doris Duke.
Emmie and David Patterson. Jean T. Sufferin
Tailor. Jamie and Peter Gregory. Leslie Wexner.
Cary Grant. Lord Esmond Rothermere. Jim Rogers.
Diane and John Samuels. Drue and Jack Heinz II.
Mary Wells Lawrence. Mary and Michael Carpenter.
Wendy Vanderbilt Lehman. Silvia and Dick Rich.
Charlotte and Jack Kessler. Pat and Bob Schiffer.
Jane and Robert Bendheim. Frances and Richard Borty.
Lee and Kenneth Auchincloss. Jerome Robbins.
Jean Kennedy and Stephen Smith. Katherine Graham.
Rose and Edgar Lansbury. Phyllis Dillon Collins.
Sir Rex and Lady Harrison. Olive, Lady Baillie.
Pat and William F. Buckley. Susan S. Lefferts.
Prince Serge Obolensky. Barbara and Donald
Tober. Lydia Bucht Melhado Farr Mann.
Gloria and Frank Schiff. Jean and Alfred Gwynne
Vanderbilt. Robert Schriver, Jr. Rose Kennedy.

Jean and Stephen Smith; Emilie and John Dickie; Lee and Kenneth Auchincloss;

June Singer. Dita Naylor Leland. Arabella and Nat Dame. Mr. Frances Leggett.